Pocket Guide to
Knots

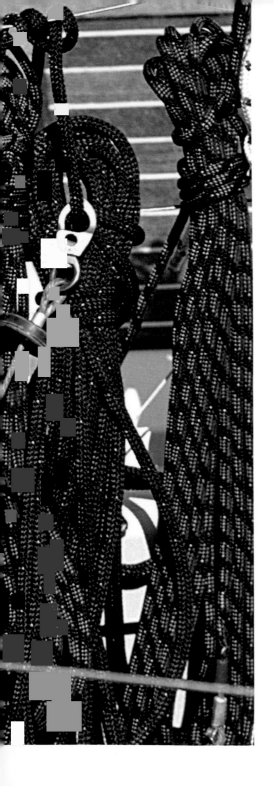

Pocket Guide to
Knots

LINDSEY PHILPOTT

International Marine / McGraw-Hill
Camden, Maine **I** New York **I**
Chicago **I** San Francisco **I** Lisbon **I**
London **I** Madrid **I** Mexico City **I**
Milan **I** New Delhi **I** San Juan **I** Seoul
I Singapore **I** Sydney **I** Toronto

The McGraw·Hill Companies

1 2 3 4 5 6 7 8 9 IMP IMP 9 8 7
Published by International Marine/McGraw-Hill
www.internationalmarine.com

First published in 2006 by New Holland Publishers Ltd

Printed and bound in Singapore.

ISBN-13: 978-0-07-149063-4
ISBN-10: 0-07-149063-9

Library of Congress Cataloging-in-Publication Data is available.

Questions regarding the content of this book should be addressed to
International Marine
P.O. Box 220
Camden, ME 04843
www.internationalmarine.com

Questions regarding the ordering of this book should be addressed to
The McGraw-Hill Companies
Customer Service Department
P.O. Box 547
Blacklick, OH 43004
Retail customers: 1-800-262-4729
Bookstores: 1-800-722-4726

Contents

Contents

This chapter offers a brief review of some of the vast history of knotting, followed by an explanation of the different types of rope and cordage that may be found, their various methods of construction, the means of coiling and caring for rope or cordage, some of the tools used in knotting and splicing, and brief definitions of the terms used. Whatever you seek in knotwork, whether you want to know a quicker way to tie your favourite knot or learn to tie one for the first time, these chapters will help you find a path through the tangles and turns to produce smooth leads and twist-free knots that perform just as intended.

ROPES

TOOLS AND TERMS

INTRODUCTION

Lucetta:	Why then, your ladyship must cut your hair.
Julia:	No, girl; I'll knit it up in silken strings,
	With twenty odd-conceited true-love knots …

(Shakespeare, The Two Gentlemen of Verona)

According to original research by archaeologist J. Wymer, there are records of knots 380,000 years old. We guess that some of the earliest held skins or thatch to the support posts of a dwelling at Terra Amata near Nice, France. From that humble beginning knotting has continued to grow becoming more complex with new materials and new discoveries.

It is almost certain that you will some day need to tie rope or cord into a knot. When you do, it is my earnest hope that you will find something in this book to help you. There are almost always more knots than you could reasonably use, but the question remains: for the situation you find yourself in right now, which knot should you use? When you find your answer here, I believe that you will be converted to thinking about knots not only on the occasion of tying the balloons for your child's birthday party, but for the sheer joy of tying string into a useful tool or decorative shape.

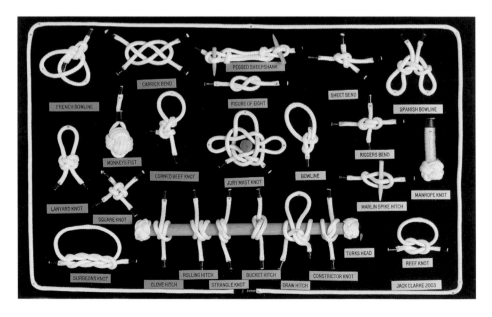

▲ Professionally tied knot boards are considered works of art by their originators.

HOW TO USE THIS BOOK

This book is arranged in sequential chapters, but if you prefer to read from the middle or end of the text, it will accommodate your immediate needs. Families of knots are grouped together in each chapter and build on what has gone before. Here are some hints to help you understand the basic layout for each knot:

- An introductory paragraph provides the history or derivation of each knot. Here, we also list alternative names for the knot and refer to others that build on, or offer interesting comparisons.
- Throughout this book we refer to the diameter of rope or line by means of the abbreviation 'd'.
- Pictographs suggest likely uses for each knot, but are not intended to be exclusive of other applications.

 sailing

 camping and outdoor pursuits

 climbing

 fishing

 decorative

 general purpose

- The photographs on each page illustrate the main steps involved in tying the knot. Follow the photographs and read the accompanying text for maximum benefit.
- If you use these knots for climbing or other hazardous pursuits, remember that you do so at your own risk. The instructions in this book are not intended as a substitute for proper instruction from a qualified instructor.
- Occasionally we provide security tips after the step-by-step text. For your own safety, follow these tips carefully!
- The tip boxes provide points to facilitate tying a knot, further uses of the knot and occasionally an alternative method of tying.
- Throughout this book, we refer to the right hand as the dominant hand and the left hand as the subdominant hand. If you are left-handed, simply use the left hand where you see references to the right hand. You can also prop this book alongside a mirror so that you can read the written material directly from the book and look at the reflected photo image to see the exact left-hand method.
- A glossary is provided in case you are not already familiar with some of the terms used.

ORIGINS, HISTORY AND USES

Humans have secured or 'lashed' one object to another throughout history. However, lashings need to be secured with knots. So, how did knots come about?

Knotting and lashing were probably first used by early *Homo erectus* (1.2 million to 400,000 years ago) to make composite tools and construct portable shelters. The techniques and tools improved with *Homo neanderthalensis* (200,000 years ago) and through the practice of hunting with bola weights in Africa and China. Remnants of this type of weapon were discovered in sites that are at least 500,000 years old.

Knots as tools were not greatly in physical evidence until after the last ice age (around 10,000 to 8000 years ago) when early man, *Homo sapiens*, became more focused on agriculture.

Knotting extended the applications of tool making, and broadened to include the practice of securing skins together to form tents, simple garments and shoes. Crafts such as fishing and weaving further developed the art of knotting and increased the need for strong, yet pliable materials that could be used to bind and tie.

The making of simple floating rafts during the Palaeolithic and Neolithic eras (between 2 million and 10,000 years ago) was highly significant for the development of rope making. Coastal and eventually transoceanic voyages

were made with coracles – vessels made from animal skins stretched over wooden frames. Seizing the craft together with sinews, leather strips and lashings of cedar bark became an art form in itself. The great age of sail, from about AD1600 through AD1900, helped to

spread and formalize knotting practices throughout the world.

For the sake of longevity, the use of leather had to be revised to make the line waterproof. New fibres and methods of treating existing fibres meant the invention of new methods to tie

▲ Racing yachts, and some modern cruising yachts like this one, are well known for their use of high-tech lines.

knots in slippery lines. The development of masted craft with sails (such as the coracle or Irish curragh) also brought about the need for standing rigging that was sturdy and able to resist the abrasion that inevitably resulted from longer journeys.

Sail trim and sail control demanded different fibres and knots that would hold in the running rigging. Today, sophisticated racing yachts drive ever greater developments in lines and knotting.

With the increased use of knotting came the need for new flexible materials that retained the tensile strength of the original material. The limitations of grasses, sinews, leather strips and other semi-flexible rope-making material gave rise to the need for an improved fibre.

Twisted groups of long grasses were found to hold together better and appeared stronger than parallel, single stalks. This technique improved the ability of the ropes to stay intact, to be flexible and to make longer ropes than were available in the natural fibre.

Cotton, silk, hemp, manila, sisal, henequen, coir and other natural products formed the earliest of the fibres for rope-like material. To a lesser extent, human and animal hair was used in practical and decorative works, but the

HISTORY'S TREASURE TROVE

The rope used 10,000 to 8000 years ago rotted away naturally, but we can find circumstantial evidence for its need:

■ The hand axe was the principal chopping tool during the middle to late Pleistocene period (between 1.8 million to 11,000 years ago). As a shaped stone held in the hand, the hand axe did not require lashing.

■ The greater leverage of the pole axe was needed to hew down trees, and to lash poles together for use in home-building and fence-making. Poles tied together made a barrier from the cold; they aided in the construction of wattle fences, and could be used for restraining domestic animals.

■ Leather strips provided strong lashings and secure fastenings in the Stone Age (2 million years ago). The development of the wheel in the later Bronze Age (approximately 3500 years ago) further reinforced the need for leather lashings to ensure flexibility of the joints in carts and war chariots. Without them, the rigid joints from regular woodwork would have resulted in many broken carts on the rough roads and byways.

idea of twisting thin fibres together was clearly significant.

The development of rope over the last hundred years or so, from the invention of wire rope in the mid 1800s and Nylon in the early 1900s, has vastly improved the art and science of knot-tying.

More recent developments over the last 30 years have included the monofilament line, the potential length of which is almost limitless; a variety of weaving techniques to improve holding power; and the reheating and pre-stretching of fibres to give improved tensile strength in the superfibres of today, where some ropes are stronger than steel wire ropes, size for size.

Functionality apart, knotting has also added to the decorative value of stone, wood, metal and glass ornamentation in churches, public buildings and family coats of arms. Celtic knot-work is one of the ornate forms of knotting used in decorating books, stone crosses, jewellery, sword hilts and leatherwork. Add to this Korean *maedup*, Chinese knotting and Japanese *hanamusubi*, and a panoply of new techniques and intricate decorative forms emerges.

The Inca *quipu*, although not particularly dec-orative, helped to cement a nation together through this vital communication and record-keeping tool.

The intricacy of knotting is intriguing to mathematicians and young children alike, who are drawn to knots with colourful names and complex forms for different reasons – think of the Turk's Head, the Monkey's Fist and the Highwayman's Hitch. Mathematicians enjoy the possibilities of examining the topology of space and time in mathematical knots and string theory. Children want to know how to tie the knots; they have little or no fear of the intricacy and see the intertwining as something to master and use for themselves.

Forensic knot analysis furthers the ability of the criminologist to determine more about the perpetrator of a crime from the ligatures used. The forensic knot analyst detects past patterns of behaviour, the tyer's handedness, and some-times also the speed or haste of the knot-tyer's actions. This information can provide vital clues to help criminologists track down the perpetrator.

Knotting can save lives in the form of a surgeon's sutures or the use of free-rope tech-niques by search-and-rescue teams. Knotting also has its place in aerospace (control wires), building (lashing scaffolding poles), book-binding, camping, climbing, decorating and fashion (macrame), electrical installation (pulling cables), engineering (bridges and cranes), fish-ing, garrotes, horse tack, knotted decorations, lariats, needlework, spelunking (caving), tatting, whips, xebecs and zithers, to name a few!

Ropes have progressed adeptly from natural fibres, such as lianas and grasses, to woven and heat-treated fibres made from oil-derived plastics. They now include in their families such types as twisted wire ropes with flat outer surfaces for elevator cables, coated braided fibre lines that resist abrasion and shock loading for rock climbing, tapes of steel or plastics for binding packages together, and extruded plastics of monofilament construction for long-line commercial fishing. Here are some of the main types of line used today:

- Monofilament construction utilizes extruded plastics to form a single-thickness material that is flexible, light and readily coiled to form fishing line that may be several miles long with no splices or knots! Specialized monofilament lines even include tapered and coloured construction for fly-fishing – the lines are light and practically invisible to the fish. Monofilament is also the basis of the more complex multifilament ropes. Steel-wire rope comprises preformed monofilament wires twisted into strands and ropes. However, this wire is drawn through a die and is not extruded.

- Twisted rope fibres produce a homogeneous and flexible material that can be produced consistently and economically, yet still retain

White 3-strand right-laid twisted nylon line

Extruded monofilament nylon line

6-strand wire with Independent Wire Rope Core (6x19 IWRC), pictured here with exposed core

8-strand multi-plait nylon

8-strand single-braided (plaited) polypropylene

16-strand double-braided polyester cover over 16-strand braided polyester core (pictured here with exposed core)

▲ 12-strand single-braided urethane-coated Spectra™, known as Spectron 12 by Samson Ropes™

▲ 24-strand braided polyester cover over 16-strand braided multifilament polypropylene/Spectra™ core, known as Samson's XLS Extra™

▲ 8-strand braided heatset multifilament polypropylene over 5-strand parallel fibre core

▲ 4-strand left-laid twisted hemp fibre

▲ 3-strand right-laid twisted sisal fibre

▲ Red, white and blue polypropylene worming added to a length of 3-strand polypropylene Roblon™ (treated with UV-resistant coating)

▲ Nylon webbing

the feel of the original plant source. Twisting the fibres together produces nearly parallel fibres in individual strands which, in turn, can be twisted into rope. Twisted fibre rope is probably the oldest form of tool still in use today, apart from the lever.

■ Braided lines have a composite construction made possible by the use of man-made materials of continuous length that are formed into two or more parts. These parts work together to provide abrasion-resistant materials that are also resistant to massive dynamic, tensile and torsion forces.

■ Twisted wire ropes are flexible (with many layers) and abrasion resistant (with fewer layers of thicker wire) for continuous use as cables in control surfaces of airplanes, spacecraft or even the common lift.

■ Tapes of fibre or metal have found great utility in a world that demands the securing together of square or cubic forms, such as boxes on pallets. The knots and fastenings used to secure cubic forms have been developed along with those new materials.

Today's vast array of ropes and cordage is a far cry indeed from the days of sinews and grasses, and yet ropes still use the power of resisting the elemental forces of tension and torsion, just as steel plates resist the elemental forces of compression and shearing.

types of rope, cordage and tape

The three basic materials used in rope making are the use of spun or extruded monofilament, twisted multifilament, and braided multifilament. Tapes are produced by a combination of braiding, weaving or by extrusion as a ribbon. The long fibres of the base material lend themselves to spinning or weaving processes that can produce longer yarns, strands and ropes.

Because not all fibres have the same length, however, it is necessary to use different spinning, twisting and weaving techniques to produce the desired length, springiness, tensile strength, abrasion resistance, flexibility and ability to accept knots.

Despite the use of so many man-made fibres, some ropes are still made from natural fibres. Natural fibres have a better 'feel' or 'hand' when used for lines aboard ships, for use in the garden or for restraining horses and other large animals. Combinations of the three techniques are used to make a wider variety of lines today than was ever possible in the past.

Monofilament line is produced from molten material that hardens on cooling. The material is squeezed through a spinneret to produce a fine, thread-like line commonly used in specialized applications such as fishing and open-heart surgery. Product consistency is maintained by ensuring that the original temperature remains within fine limits, while not burning the product with high-speed production methods. Because the resulting monofilament is stiff, it requires the use of cold crimping through rollers to produce a more flexible line.

THREE-STRAND LINE

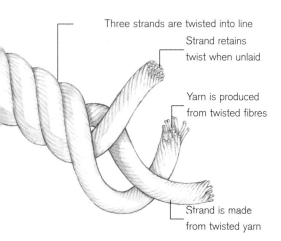

Three strands are twisted into line

Strand retains twist when unlaid

Yarn is produced from twisted fibres

Strand is made from twisted yarn

BRAIDED-COVER TWISTED-CORE LINE

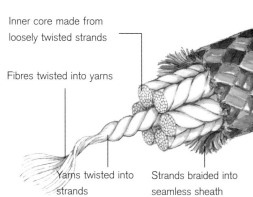

Inner core made from loosely twisted strands

Fibres twisted into yarns

Yarns twisted into strands

Strands braided into seamless sheath

Twisted or laid multifilament line uses the process of twisting large numbers of the original fine fibres in parallel into a series of yarns. The yarns are twisted together in the opposing direction to form strands. The resulting strands are then twisted in the opposing direction again to form line. The resulting twisted line is formed either as Z-twist (right laid) or as S-twist (left laid) for use in the appropriate location. When twisting the original fibres together in this fashion, they form strong bonds between the original fibres. The developed twist and countertwist together help to prevent the 'unlaying' or 'unravelling' of a line.

Multifilament line is produced by combining several dozen strands of very thin monofilaments

▲ The manufacture of rope in the mid-18th century was a laborious process, as depicted in this engraving dated approximately 1760.

into a thicker thread that is then used as the basis for weaving a new line. Braided multifilament line is produced by taking several yarns of parallel multi-fibres and then weaving them into a homogeneous line using a 'maypole' over-and-under construction.

Plain-braid, braid-on-braid or braid-on-laid and braid-on-parallel constructions are the four principal methods used for constructing special-purpose ropes. Plain- or single-braided line is made by forming a tube of maypole construction

how ropes are made   19

without a core. Braided line is typically made with comparatively few yarns (8-, 12-, or 16-strand line) plaited together to form a continuous tubular form of line. Braid-on-braid is formed by making a tube of braided cover or sheath material over a core of simply braided yarns. Braid-on-laid is made by using a tube of braided line to cover a laid (twisted-line) core. Parallel-fibre construction uses a tube of braided line to cover a core of parallel-fibre yarns parcelled with light paper or tape.

The materials used in construction of lines are almost as varied as the lines themselves. Natural and man-made fibres form the basis of all line materials.

Some of the more popular sources of natural fibre include silk (from silkworms, *Bombyx mori*), cotton (from the cotton plant *Gossypium hirsutum*), sisal and henequen (from the *Agave sisalana* and the *Agave fourcroydes* plants), manila (from *Musa textilis*), coir (from *Cocos nucifera*), hemp (from *Cannabis sativa*), linen (from *Linum usitatissimum*), as well as jute and seagrass. However, natural fibres are gradually giving way to man-made materials of a more consistent quality.

All man-made fibre ropes comprise either plastics or metals. The plastics include four basic polymers – polyamide (PA-6 or nylon), polyester (Terylene or Dacron), polyethylene (polythene), and polyolefins (polypropylene). Other plastics are formed from the basic polymers, such as Kevlar (from aramids), Polysteel (from co-polymers of polystyrene and polypropylene), low-creep Vectran (from liquid crystal polymer), Spectra (from ultra-high molecular-weight polyethylene), and Technora (another aramid but with improved fatigue life).

The drawn metals, such as iron, steel, stainless steel, copper, bronze and aluminium, also have different applications for ropes. Most metal ropes cannot be knotted because they are stiff. However, we include them here because all can be spliced or joined by cable connectors.

◀ A rope-twisting machine used in World War I and during the Great Depression in Iowa, USA, to make ropes from twine and lightning conductors from wire for agricultural use.

ropes – tools and terms

Like most tools, each type of rope and cordage (the line and rigging of a vessel) requires specific maintenance, storage and care. You can usually obtain this information from the original manufacturer for specific applications. Generally, however, ropes and cordage will last much longer if these few simple techniques are incorporated into their maintenance programme:

■ Keep dirt away from and out of the line. Dirt particles will wear away your line from the inside and create a hidden danger for lines that are highly or dynamically loaded.

■ Whip the ends of your lines before washing to prevent them from fraying and forming an unsightly cow's tail. This means making tightly made turns around the ends (see pp176–181).

■ Wash your ropes coiled in a laundry bag with little or no (mild) detergent. I have successfully used a quarter capful of fabric softener in an otherwise clean washing machine to produce clean lines that perform under load for well over five years. Stop the

▲ Lines hung in gasket coils dry well and are easier to locate for immediate use.

machine during the first cycle to allow the line to soak for about 25 or 30 minutes to aid the washing process. I suggest that you repeat this washing procedure every three to five years depending on how dirty the line becomes.

- To ensure a longer life for your fibre rope, hang the coils out of sunlight, in a place with plenty of air circulation to avoid the onset of mildew and mould. Do not under any circumstances use a dryer to dry your lines!

- Rinse them occasionally. Rinsing your lines with fresh water if they have been dunked in seawater during use (accidentally of course!) will help to keep them clean. Hang them out to dry as detailed above. If you never manage to dunk your lines, rinse them with fresh water once every six months or so, depending on use.

Standing or fixed rigging lines to support masts are made of wire cable and should also be rinsed occasionally after use. Many years ago, I had the unfortunate instance of stepping on a stainless steel line that was being used as a footrope, only to have it break under me. Unbeknown to me, chloride corrosion had steadily eaten away at the wires at the point

of their swaging. A simple rinsing of the swaging would have prevented the accumulation of salts and corrosion. Now I visually check every line before use.

- Keep tidy. Always coil a line after use, so that it is immediately ready for the next use. If you cannot coil the line, at least fold it in half, then half again and half again for temporary storage until the line can be more easily coiled.

- Never overload your lines! Dynamic or shock loading of your line occurs when you add a load suddenly, such as dropping a tied load through even a few feet. If you dynamically load a line beyond its stated limit, you will overstretch and weaken the line and it will not recover. Shock loading will severely compromise your lines and could result in personal damage or death!

ropes – tools and terms

Because your rope is your lifeline its physical integrity should be maintained at all times during handling, particularly when coiled, carried or stored. Here are a few guidelines to follow:

- Coils of line are much easier to carry than a tangled heap, and easier to use because the line is readily accessible. The alpine coil has been used for nearly a century and is very useful as a storage method or for carrying lines when climbing.

- Coil ropes with their original lay. Right-laid rope should be coiled clockwise, left-laid rope anticlockwise. Braided line may be coiled in either direction, but consistently each time or it will develop kinks (hockles) or snarls (twists and tangles) that can weaken the fibres of both core and sheath.

- Stop or tie bands around coils. Coiled ropes will be less likely to tangle if stopped by tying at three points around the coil's perimeter with small pieces of twine. Tie the ends of each stop with a slipped Reef Knot (p158) to bundle the coil's parts together at each point. The stops are then readily untied when you need the coil. Use wire if you are stopping wire rope. If the line is used regularly and stopping is not feasible, try some of the coiling techniques shown in the photographs below.

- If you regularly carry or use coils of multi-strand wire you may also find it useful to remember to lubricate your line periodically in accordance with manufacturer's directions, but remember never to lubricate a fibre line!

◄ Gasket coil (opposite), Stopped coil and Alpine coil (above left and right).

■ Keep coils of line away from chemicals. Oils, acids, alkalis, petroleum or other chemicals will reduce the line's properties, so store them away from wire or fibre ropes. Also keep coils of line away from excessive heat and cold. To prevent abrasion, don't store metal tools on top of coils that are laid flat, and ensure that adjacent coils are free to the air.

■ Storage recommendations for wire ropes are very similar to those of fibre ropes. Dry and clean storage is best where the coils can be hung or, for wire, laid flat. Store wire ropes and fibre ropes sepa-rately to avoid possible cross-contamination. Tying stops around the perimeter of each coil will permit easy selection when the ropes are needed.

Many different tools have been used over the years to assist the rope maker and worker, par-ticularly when splicing or weaving the strands of the rope together. Many of these have changed little over time, simply because there is no per-ceived need to improve their functional design.

One of the simplest tools for rope working is the fid. Fids are generally used to separate the individual strands in laid rope, or to thread the cover and core when splicing braided rope. Needles used in sail-making have been pressed into use for rope working also. The tri-angular shape of sail-making needles enables a smooth transition through the twisted or braided fibres to enable strong, sewn connec-tions. Use of a leather palm helps to guide the needle through the sailcloth or through the rope when whipping. The tool fits over the entire hand and is fitted

◀ From left to right: a sailmaker's palm, sheath knife, and needle case. The sheath knife and needle case are handsomely covered with half-hitching and Turk's Head decora-tive ropework, collectively known as marlinespike seamanship.

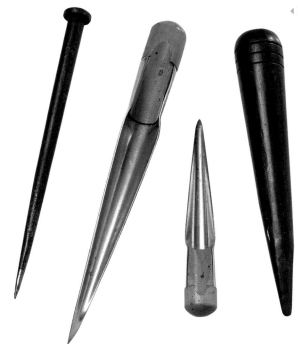

◄ From left to right: marlinespike, two Swedish fids and a wooden fid. The marlinespike is used to splice wire ropes, while the fids are used to splice fibre ropes and to open knots.

with a metal thimble. The sewing-needle eye fits into the thimble and the needle is gripped with finger and thumb, so that it can be pushed through the line or fabric using the force and momentum of the entire arm, not just the strength of the fingers.

Twisted rope-making tools include gyratory twisting machines like those used by farmers during World War I and the Great Depression in America (p20). Using skeins of cheap sisal twine, they were able to make a substitute rope for many agricultural needs when manila and hemp ropes were scarce.

Needle-nosed pliers help to tighten fishing knots that have been made with mono-filament line. Also very helpful is the use of forceps, either straight or bent, especially when making a Blood Knot, Monkey's Fist or a similar knot.

Netting needles help to keep large quanti-ties of twine under control when making or mending netting. They have a cut-out section, allowing fishing net twine to be loaded in the centre for repair. Netting needles also help to store the twine from an otherwise readily flat-tened ball of it.

BASIC TYING TECHNIQUES

Throughout this book we refer to the working end and standing part of a line. The working end of a line is that part which is being passed or used in the formation of the knot, while the standing part is that part which is not being used. Many of the terms used in this introduction are explained in greater detail in the glossary, together with other specialist terms. Here are some helpful hints for working with line:

■ Always remember that, when you are taking line from a ball of twine, you should start from the inside so the ball stays together.

■ When taking line from a box of line pull from the inside of the coil without taking the coil out of the box. Then take anticlockwise turns for the length you need. Recoil the line clockwise, again starting from the centre, so that the line does not form kinks.

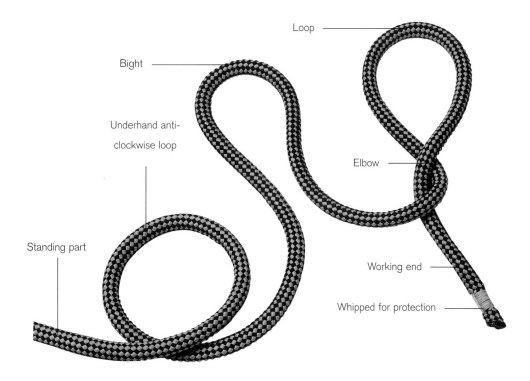

Loop

Bight

Underhand anti-
clockwise loop

Elbow

Standing part

Working end

Whipped for protection

- Wire rope should never be taken from the inside of a coil. Mount the coil so that it can rotate freely, then unwind the wire as it was wound on. Pull the wire to rotate the coil, otherwise it has a tendency to kink and has to be discarded.

- If you are using a long length of twine, it can be formed into a hank by winding the line onto the outstretched thumb and little finger of one hand in a figure-eight pattern. When you have nearly reached the end of the line, form a Clove Hitch around the hank (fox) in the 'waist' of the figure eight, and pull the cord from the starting end only. Retighten the final Clove Hitch (p72) as the line is used up.

- Use masking tape to temporarily whip the end of your line, in other words before forming a proper whipped end. Tape will also prevent individual strands from unlaying when working with a three-strand line. I have also used tape to mark the beginning of a splice, or to number the lines being made into a sinnet (a form of braiding).

- Use a butane lighter to melt the ends of synthetic line, to prevent it from fraying. Some synthetics require less heat than others, so be careful not to burn the material. You can do this by using a test piece first.

- When pulling on a line, never wrap it around your palm or hand as it can become entangled and you will likely suffer damage to your hand. If you need to pull with a force greater than you can exert with your hand and fingers alone, consider using a temporary sling, a winch or a Marlinespike Hitch (p93).

Are you ready for the journey through knots, bends, hitches, loops, bindings, plaits and other special knots? Join me now in a quick trip through the line fantastic! Perhaps you will become another of the great knot tyers of this world!

◁ To tie and apply the knots in this book effectively ensure you have grasped the basic terms referring to the respective parts and configurations of rope. Once you have familiarized yourself with these terms, you will be able to easily identify which part of a rope is being used at a particular stage of tying a knot.

Stopper knots are usually formed in the end of a piece of line to create a structure that prevents the line from moving through a restriction. This family of knots is also useful when you do not want to use a loop knot as a terminal to your line.

Many more stopper knots exist than the few shown here, and they all perform elegantly. Beware of tying the simpler forms in expensive line, however, because the result may ruin perfectly good rope. Occasionally people follow the old maxim 'If you can't tie the right knot, tie lots', thinking that they are improving their chances of securing a load. Beware of following this advice; you can severely reduce the tensile strength of your line by tying too many knots.

STOPPER KNOTS

Overhand Knot

This stopper knot can be formed in monofilament as easily as it can in polyester braided line. Its greatest value is that it is large, easily remembered and difficult to tie wrongly. Its greatest weakness, however, is that it is not easy to untie if it has been tightened down under load, perhaps requiring a fid to open it. Use the knot wherever you need a more or less permanent stop to the end of your line.

1. Form an overhand loop, taking the working end in a clockwise direction over the standing part.

2. Now pass the working end into the loop from below, making a single Overhand Knot. Pull through sufficient line at the working end to finish the knot.

3. To form a Double Overhand Knot, pass the working end through the loop a second time. For a Triple Overhand Knot, pass the working end through a third time to complete the structure.

4. Finally, fair the knot by pulling on the working end and the standing part, making sure that all twists are tucked neatly into the knot. A Double Overhand Knot is shown here, made fair.

Variation: Tied with a Draw Loop

The addition of a draw loop makes the Overhand Knot easier to untie (Slippery Overhand Knot). Draw loops should be used with caution, however. If the parts of the loop taken into the knot are laid over one another, they may make the knot weaker. Instead, lay them alongside each other prior to tightening. This stopper may be used on the fly-sheet grommet for quick-release or on a sheet stopped at the fairlead.

1. Start the knot with an overhand loop formed clockwise. Leave a long enough working end so that the draw loop or bight can be formed with the remaining working end.

2. Form a bight in an anticlockwise direction, so that the working end is not crossing over the bight. Insert the bight up into the first loop formed.

Tips

This knot is readily undone, no matter how big the draw loop or bight. Adjust the size of the draw loop for your needs; never place any load in the loop itself.

3. Fair the knot. Draw it up tight enough for the intended use. The tail or working end will lie out to one side if you have faired the knot sufficiently.

Double Diamond Knot

A succession of Double Diamond knots, used as large stoppers in three-strand line, was originally used in jib-boom footropes to help sailors maintain their footing along wet or icy footropes and prevent them from slipping. The knot is now more usually applied in the end of a lanyard. Tied in the working end, it prevents the lanyard from slipping through the hole in the end of a marlinespike, for instance.

1. Unlay the strands of a laid line for about 50d. Form three bights and put an elastic band around the tails to hold them as shown.

2. Pass strand #1 over the tail of strand #2 and tuck it up into the bight of strand #3.

3. Pass strand #2 over the tail of strand #3 and tuck it up into the bight of strand #1.

4. Repeat Steps 2 and 3 for the final strand.

5. Fair the knot to bring all the strands up through the bights loosely.

6. Follow the lead of strand #1 with its own working end, doubling it down under its own strand and parallel to it.

This knot can either be tied with each strand parallel to and below its own part, or parallel to and above its own part. To finish it, relay the emerging strands together and apply a whipping (pp176–81) of your choice.

7. Repeat Step 6 with strand #2, being sure to keep the knot centre open.

8. Repeat with strand #3, and observe the triangle of double strands on top of the knot.

9. Pass strand #3, parallel to its own part, up into the centre of the triangle.

10. Repeat Step 9 with strand #2 and then with strand #1, to bring all three strands together.

11. Fair the knot by following each strand in turn, and tightening each strand gradually.

double diamond knot   33

Figure-of-Eight Knot

An addition of one or more twists to the Overhand Knot forms the Figure-of-Eight or Flemish Knot. When you form it, do not stop after you have made the initial shape. When the working end is at right angles to the standing part, the knot is made 'nice'. Remember this rhyme: 'Twist it once, twist it twice; pass it through and make it nice' to fair the knot at the end and so make it work correctly. This knot may be used to stop a line through a cleat, or a Clove Hitch (p72) from being undone.

1. Make an overhand loop with the working end (in this photo it is formed clockwise).

2. Twist the line under the standing part, to move it from the front to the back of the standing part. Here the loop has been twisted under and away from you.

3. Pass the working end up into the loop to complete the third step of this knot.

4. Push the knot toward the working end holding the standing part with your right hand and then pulling away from the knot with the left.

5. The working end will now project at right angles to the standing part.

Tips

Remembering to fair up this knot will be of benefit only if the knot is used in a static position. If it is likely to be suddenly and heavily dynamically loaded, don't fair it up, because this final tightening, due to sudden load, will help absorb some of the shock. However, you should then also leave a longer working end of at least 10d in length.

Heaving Line Knot

As its name implies, the Heaving Line Knot is used to heave a line to a distant point that cannot be reached by simply throwing the line itself. The alternative name, Franciscan Knot, probably derives from the similarity to the tassel-like knot on the monks' habit. To avoid the damage that may result from throwing heavy objects tied to the end of the line, use this knot, quickly formed and readily undone, when you are camping and need to get a line over a branch to tie up your food away from wild animals! If you are trying to get a heavy hawser to the shore, or intend to attach another line to the distant end of the line, use a Sheet Bend (p106) to haul the heavier line.

1. Form a bight in the end of your heaving line – about 600mm (24in) in length – depending on its thickness. At about 250mm (10in) away from the bight, start wrapping the working end around the parts of the bight. Work toward the end of the bight and make your first pass lock down over itself.

2. Continue making turns around the parts of the bight until you have used up all the line. Be sure that each wrap is tightened as you go, to ensure maximum density in the finished knot.

3. Tuck the working end through the last visible part of the bight and then pull down on the standing part to tighten the bight onto the working end. Voilà! Your knot is completed.

Tips

To make a heavier line, use a doubled bight and complete the same steps as above, tucking the working end through both parts of the end of the bight. Do be sure to keep your wraps tight.

Wall Knot

The Wall Knot is usually found alongside the Crown Knot, forming decorative structures or finishing the ends of ropes. The Wall Knot can also be used to form sennit work, to make bell-ropes or to plait rope forms. Walling a series of lines together will produce a really lumpy surface that is good for gripping. Walling and crowning the end of a man-overboard rope will give a good handhold.

1. Unlay the strands of a laid rope, and number them anticlockwise. Take line #1 around your upraised thumb and under line #2 and hold upright.

2. Pass strand #2 around your thumb and over strand #1.

3. Take line #2 around line #3 and hold it upright like the first line. Now you have two lines up in the air, with line #3 hanging down.

4. Bring line #3 up through the bight of line #1 that is around your thumb, then remove your thumb. You now should have all three lines in the air as shown.

5. Finish the knot by fairing each line individually, being careful not to pull any one line too tight, or the knot will distort. Repeat as needed.

Tips

The main difference between the Wall Knot and the Crown Knot is the direction in which the lines are passed – remember that a 'wall' is built up, whereas 'crown' rhymes with down. Hence, the Wall Knot strands each come up through the knot.

Crown Knot

The Crown Knot is used in combination with the Wall Knot (left) to form a finishing 'knob' at the end of a Manrope (p40). The Crown Knot is also the basis of forming a Crown Sinnet and several other fancy knots. As a stopper knot, the Crown Knot cannot be used by itself, and must be combined with either a Wall Knot or with splicing to form the end of a line (pp170–5).

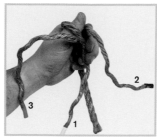

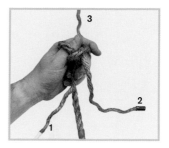

1. Unlay the three strands to the point where you would like to form the Crown Knot. Drafting tape will prevent the line as well as the individual strands from unlaying any further.

2. Place your thumb at the junction of the strands, applying pressure to hold them apart. Fold strand #1 over your thumb and over strand #3, to form a bight over your thumb.

3. Fold strand #3 over strand #2, so that you repeat what happened with strand #1. Strand #3 now lies over strand #2 and points down like strand #1.

4. While removing your thumb, pass strand #2 over strand #3 and under strand #1 where your thumb was. Each strand now lies between two others.

5. Remove the drafting tape and fair the knot by pull-ing on the working end of each strand to form a tight triangle.

Tips

If you are forming a Crown Sennit using more than four unpaired strands, you will need to put a core in the centre of all the strands or the knot will collapse. Remember, the word 'crown' rhymes with the word 'down', which is the direction in which the individual strands are taken for each pass. Try using a Constrictor Knot (p142) instead of the drafting tape mentioned in Step 1.

Double Matthew Walker Knot

⚓ 🎁

The legend I have heard about the Double Matthew Walker Knot is that Walker was sentenced to death for crimes he allegedly committed on the high seas. The judge, a former sailor, told Walker that he would go free if he could tie a knot that the judge could neither tie nor untie. Matthew duly tied this knot in the middle of a piece of line – and the good judge was forced let him go free. The knot can be used as a permanent stopper in the lanyards that hold up the shrouds and guys of those lovely old square-riggers, now alas so seldom seen. It makes for a very solid and elegant two-strand knot on the tails of a zipper pull also.

1. The knot can be started by tying a loose Wall Knot (p36), but be sure to label or mark the ends of each strand with coloured tape. It helps to put a tight piece of drafting tape around the line where you are starting the Wall Knot. This is right-laid line, so the ends of the strands are laid anticlockwise.

2. Now tuck strand #1 in an anticlockwise fashion to follow around strand #2 lying next to it.

3. Follow strand #2 exactly. Hold down strand #1 against the rope, out of the way. Fair the knot, but do not pull it tight yet!

This knot can also be tied by first tying an Overhand Knot (p30) with each strand around the standing part of the knot (anticlockwise for right-laid strands). The working end of each Overhand Knot will pass through the loop of the preceding Overhand Knot. All working ends will thus end up having passed through all preceding Overhand Knots. The greatest number of strands that I have ever seen tied in this fashion is 104, tied by International Guild of Knot Tyers' member, Harold Scott.

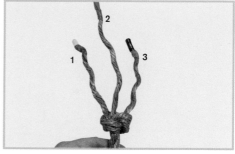

4. Now repeat Steps 2 and 3 for each strand, so that you end up with three twice-tucked strands. Again, fair the knot so that all the strands lie adjacent to each other. You will see that each strand now lies such that it is an Overhand Knot with the working end sticking up through it.

5. Fair for the last time, pulling each strand up and over its neighbour, so that it appears as above. Press each strand into the body of the knot to fair it. The finished knot, if started in right-laid line, will now appear to be left laid, each strand starting from the lower right to finish at the upper left-hand side of the knot when viewed from the side.

6. If desired, remove the tape from Step 1, and then trim the ends of the strands, so that only a short length of strand emerges from the top of the knot. You could also re-lay the line back up into its original form, thereby mystifying anyone who thinks of undoing it.

Manrope Knot

'First a Wall, then a Crown, next go up, then go down' goes the rhyme young sailors would learn to remember how to make the Manrope Knot. This knot is a modification of an earlier, very similar knot called the Tack Knot, which dates to about 1794 in Darcy Lever's book. Being able to tie this knot will mark you as a competent knot tyer. Try it with different coloured lines so that you can see the shape develop.

1. Form a Wall Knot (p36), leaving each strand at least 250mm (10in) long.

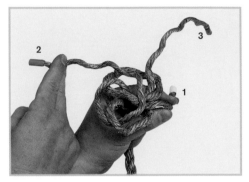

2. Form each strand in turn into a Crown Knot (p37). Strand #2 is shown here being passed.

3. Each strand now lies above its first pass, ready for the second pass.

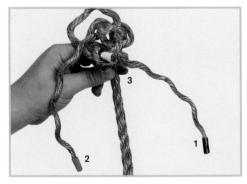

4. Pass strand #1 above and parallel to its own part, up into the knot.

5. Repeat Step 4 with strands #2 and #3. This completes the line 'next go up'.

6. Pass strand #1 parallel alongside its own part down into the knot.

7. Repeat Step 6 with strands #2 and #3. This completes the last line of the rhyme 'then go down'. Fair the knot and trim the ends.

8. Fair the knot and trim the ends.

Stopper Knot

The Stopper Knot is used as an alternative to the Heaving Line Knot (p35) where you need a heavier weight at the end of a line. It is a little more difficult to tie, but adds weight to the end of your line. Do not be too hasty in tying this knot – patience is a great virtue here!

1. First take the line across the fingers of your subdominant hand (left hand in this picture for a right-handed person) and wind it from front to back around the tips of your fingers.

2. Continue making turns all the way down your fingers until you have only enough line to slip through the knot up to the tips of your fingers. Be careful not to make the wraps too tight.

3. Work the turns carefully off your fingers. By twisting all the turns together and holding the working end of the line in your right hand, twist all the turns until they come tightly around the Overhand Knot that lies inside the knot. This is easier if you pull the standing part at the same time as you twist the turns, thereby taking up the slack generated from the twisting.

4. Continue twisting the turns and pulling the standing part until the knot is faired down and tight around the Overhand Knot. There you have it!

Tips

When you make this knot in 11mm (0.4in) polyester cord, make the turns around a bunch of smooth twigs or some pencils instead of your fingers. When you take the turns off, the space remaining will be enough to insert the working end of your rope.

Stevedore Knot

When raising cargo to or from a ship's hold, a larger sheave (grooved wheel in pulley system) is used in the cargo block to spread the load better and give lower friction. With a larger sheave in the cargo block, a larger stopper knot is needed to prevent the line from unreeving. The Stevedore Knot fits the bill handsomely. Today, it is also used to ensure that a line does not move through a block, a fairlead or the grommet in a tarpaulin.

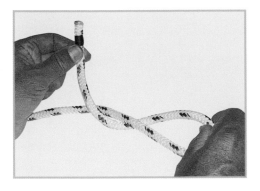

1. Start to form a Figure-of-Eight Knot (p34) in the end of your line. Do not make the final pass through.

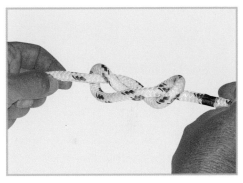

2. Wrap the working end a second time around the standing part, and then make the final pass through the top of the knot, just as you would for a Figure-of-Eight.

3. Fair the knot down as shown in the picture, by pulling the standing part to lock down the working end.

Tips

If you are using this knot for fishing, try wetting the monofilament line prior to tightening it to ease the turns into the knot.

Looped knots create structures that may be tied to another object or line. They are not the exclusive tool of the climber, mariner or even steeplejack, however, but one of the most versatile knot-tying tools available to all. The variety of looped knots is large, as you will see from the following collection of favourites. Looped knots are combination knots applied for a single purpose, yet they may be used over and again for that purpose without having to be retied. They are more varied, stronger and longer-wearing, generally speaking, than bends and hitches.

LOOPS

Alpine Butterfly Loop

An elegant knot that is simple in construction deserves first place, particularly when that knot is also able to provide life-saving service! The Alpine Butterfly Loop or Lineman's Loop serves this purpose and deserves that nomination. Used extensively in climbing, the loop adds tremendously to the helpfulness of knots because it is tied so quickly and yet holds so firmly, whether in the middle of or at the end of a line. It may also be used to isolate a defective piece of line or to provide a strong tie-in to a line for climbers strung together.

1. Pass the working end of the line over your hand. If you are using the line in the middle, simply pass it over the hand.

2. Form a second and then a third pass over the hand, so that you now have three turns over and around the hand.

3. Bring the entire inside loop over the other two, toward the fingertips.

4. Bring it over the other two again, so that the original middle loop is over the first and third loops. Tuck this last loop under the first two and back toward the thumb.

5. Pull the middle loop out through the middle of the other loops after sliding it off the hand, then fair the knot.

6. Tighten by pulling firmly on each side.

Angler's Loop

Also known as the Perfection Loop, this knot ties well in bungee cord. It is also readily tied in monofilament as a leader or tippet in fishing and is claimed to be near perfection because of its ability to hold in slippery or elastic line. The knot may be tied left-handed or right-handed, and may also be tied in the bight. It is less suitable for large diameter line (larger than 25mm; 1in) because that size of line does not adapt well to the multiple twists and turns. This knot is difficult to untie after taking a strain, so be certain that you need it before you use it.

1. Form an overhand loop anti-clockwise, with the standing part kept to the right.

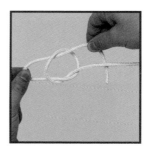

2. Pass the working end over the loop, clockwise to form a second loop, then …

3. … bring a bight of the working end out through the first loop.

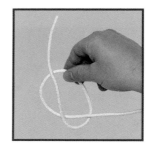

4. Pull the bight out through the first loop. Fair the knot by adjusting the length of the bight to the desired size.

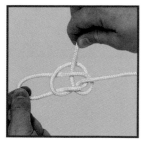

5. Pass the working end under the bight and over the first loop parts.

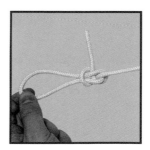

6. The working end must be pulled tight into the crossing parts, leaving a tail length of about 6d.

Blood Loop Dropper Knot

J A 🏠

The Blood Loop Dropper Knot is popular with anglers as a method of tying a loop in a leader for attaching a dropper (or a second fly), using an Angler's Loop (p47) with a lure or hook on the other end of the dropper. A supplier of kitefishing technology, Paul's Fishing Kites of New Zealand has come up with a new method of weaving the loop, which appears to work very well even in thicker monofilament. Also have a look at the Tips below for a third method. If you are using this knot in thicker line, it forms a useful method of quickly making a secure loop in the middle of the line, although it may be difficult to fair the knot and to undo it after it has taken a strain.

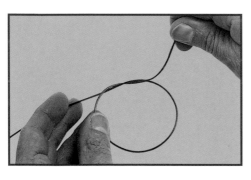

1. Form an Overhand Knot (p30) in a length of monofilament.

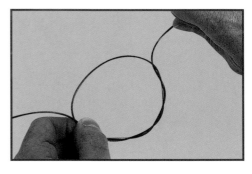

2. Make a second pass and then a third with the working end to form a Triple Overhand Knot (p30).

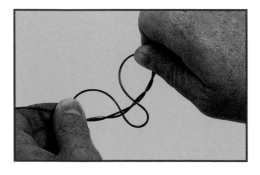

3. Use the untwisted part of the knot to form a bight. Push it through the middle of the twisted parts.

4. The knot should be wet to help it slide into place while pulling on the ends of the line. In monofilament put the loop over a peg while pulling the ends.

Jury Mast Knot

A life-saver at sea in an emergency, the Jury Mast Knot may be used simply to replace a fitting at the head of the mast that normally receives the shrouds and stays. When a mast is broken and has to be restepped on deck, this knot forms three attaching loops and a fourth set of lines for the remaining stay when tightened around the head of the new or replacement spar. As a decorative knot it can readily be formed from this simple method. The knot is known as a Pitcher Knot when it is used to hold and carry a jar or pitcher.

1. Form an underhand anticlockwise loop in the line.

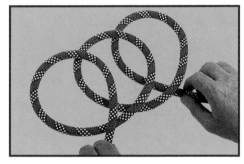

2. Form two more loops, identical to the first. Tuck each succeeding loop under the preceding one, working towards the right.

3. Reach under the right-most loop part and over the right part of the centre loop to hold the right-most part of the first loop.

4. Reach over the left-most loop part and under the left part of the centre loop to hold the left-most part of the third loop.

5. Now draw the two loops out to each side.

6. Pull the top loop out of the upper part of the knot, using the two parts of the line to pull downward.

7. Make the loops even, placing the masthead in the centre of the knot. The top loop may be used for the head stay, the side loops for the shrouds and the two line parts connected for the back stay.

Tips

The loops may be formed as two overhand loops on the outer loops and an underhand loop on the centre loop if desired, but the final form will be different. The technique remains the same: you weave the side loops over and under the other loops.

Bowline Loop

The bowline is a series of lines often toggled to the weather-edge cringles of a square sail on a square-rigged ship to keep that edge flying clear. The Bowline Loop, sometimes also referred to as the Bowline Knot, is the knot used to tie those lines together as a bridle. In modern use, the Bowline Loop is used to attach a sheet to the clew of a sail, a fall to the becket of a block, or to tie a temporary loop in the end of the dock line for passing over a dock cleat or bollard. This simple knot has a multitude of uses and variations, and is easy to untie, no matter how much strain has been put on the line.

1. With the standing part in your left hand and the working end below, make a figure 'six'. The length of the working end should be enough to make the loop and pass behind the standing part. Hold the anticlockwise overhand loop open with your left thumb.

2. Pass the working end up through the loop, being sure not to pull it through all the way. The bight below the number 'six' is the temporary loop you are making.

3. Pass the working end behind the standing part and back down into the loop from the front anti-clockwise, so that it is parallel with the first pass through the loop.

4. Hold the working end against the right part of the loop you have formed and pull on the standing part to tighten.

Variation 1: Tying around Yourself

1. Pass the working end around your waist, keeping the standing part in your left hand.

2. With the working end in your right hand (palm down), cross the standing part from right to left, close to the body.

3. Bring your right hand (palm up) toward your heart inside the standing part, so that a loop forms around your wrist.

4. The fingers of your right hand pass the working end behind the standing part from your right to left and regrip the working end above the standing part.

5. Throw the loop around your wrist off onto the standing part and tighten the knot by pulling the standing part with your left hand.

Variation 2: Tying to your Harness

1. Pass the working end through your harness loop and hold it with your right hand.

2. Rotate your left hand palm down toward your heart to form an anticlockwise overhand loop with the standing part.

3. Reach up through the left-hand loop and pull a bight of the standing part down toward you through the loop.

4. Pass the working end through the bight (front to back) pulling through sufficiently to make the tail of the bowline loop. Hold the working end.

5. Pull up on the standing part to pull the bight in the working end up through the first loop. The knot will twist to your left as you do this.

Security

Make a Double Overhand Knot with the working end around the adjacent part of the loop to ensure that slippery line does not pull through.

Tips

To undo the Bowline, push the bight off the back of the knot to release it and make the loop loose. For sailors, this mnemonic is used to remember how to tie this knot: 'Here is the mast of the ship (the standing part) and here at the step of the mast is a hatch (form the number 'six'). The sailor (the working end) is resting below (below your hand) and feels a storm coming on. He comes up through the hatch (bring the working end up through the loop), looks anticlockwise around the mast (take the working end anticlockwise around the standing part) and dives back down through the hatch (the working end goes down through the loop) to snug himself into his bunk (hold the working end against the loop part) just before the storm hits' (pull up on the standing part to tighten).

Double Bowline

This variation of the Bowline is popular with climbers because it is claimed to have greater strength, although no numbers are provided to back up this claim. In structure it is the same as the Double Sheet Bend (p107) being made with a bight trapped inside a doubled loop. Called a Round Turn Bowline by Clifford Ashley (#1013 in *The Ashley Book of Knots*, henceforward ABOK), he states that it is 'put into stiff or slippery rope' and that it 'holds the bowline together in such a way as to lessen the danger of its capsizing'. Whatever its value, be aware that it is difficult to tie with frosty fingers and may need careful fairing after being tied.

1. Form an overhand anticlockwise loop on the left hand as for the Bowline Loop.

2. Form a second loop on top of the first one and keep your left thumb on the crossing of the double loop.

3. Pass the working end through the double loop as you would for the Bowline Loop.

4. Bring the working end around the back of the standing part and tuck it down into the double loop.

5. Fair the knot by pulling the Bowline Loop's parts and by pulling on the standing part. Be careful to ensure that the double loop is tight in all parts before loading the Double Bowline.

Bowline in the Bight

To form this knot is to use some of the better attributes of this knot family, such as security and speed of tying, with a touch of three-dimensional mind-gaming. The essential difference here is not that it is tied in the bight, but that the formed loops are static and less likely to slip around. Furthermore, each loop may be loaded separately and differently from the others, making it quite versatile. Climbers, sailors and rescue personnel alike use it because it holds well and provides a tag line for steadying the person in the sling.

1. Form a large bight in the line – by holding the bight in your right hand and standing on the doubled line – so that, with the standing parts in your left hand, both hands reach a little above your waist. Treating the pair of parts as one and holding them in your left hand, form an overhand anticlockwise loop.

2. Insert the bight up into the formed loop from below, just enough to make the desired size of finished loops.

3. Open the bight so that it is large enough to pull through the parts of the loops. In doing so you transfer the bight from the front to the back of the loop knot without cutting the line. The bight itself folds back under the first formed loop when you pull the parts through the bight.

4. Hold the formed loop tight at the crossing and fair the knot together so that you can now pull up on the standing part to close the formed loop around the bight, thus securing the loop knot.

Portuguese Bowline

When it is used as a part of a bosun's chair or other support, the Portuguese Bowline makes a more comfortable sitting position possible. The doubled loops produce a greater area for spreading the load. As a safety loop knot it should be used with caution, however, because when one loop at a time is loaded, that loop tends to slip through the knot, making the other loop smaller and tighter around the body of the person being lifted. This knot was also named the French Bowline by Felix Riesenberg in *Standing Seamanship for the Merchant Service* (1922), where it is touted as a potential safety knot.

1. Form an overhand anticlockwise loop in the standing part allowing enough line toward the working end to make a loop twice as large as you need.

2. Pass the working end through the formed loop and pull it through until you have made the desired loop size.

3. Form a second loop with the working end on top of the previous loop, again tucking the working end up through the original loop.

4. Lead the working end up around the standing part anticlockwise and back down into the formed loop.

5. Pull on the standing part to close the formed loop around the parts of the loop.

Spanish Bowline

⚓ 🔺 🔺 🏠

Being able to form a rope chair with this form of the Bowline allows for a fairly safe application. The two loops form a solid structure through which the legs are passed, resulting in the person being hoisted hanging on to the doubled parts of the standing part. The knot is made in the bight and was, at some time, known as a Double Forked Loop (*ABOK* #1087). Some slippage may occur, however, because the two loops are not independent of each other. The loops at the centre must be faired down to make the knot more slip-resistant.

1. Form a large bight in the line and allow it to fall behind the standing parts as shown, forming one clockwise and one anticlockwise overhand loop.

2. Holding the loops at the top, twist each one a half turn in toward each other.

3. Pass the left-hand loop into the open right-hand loop from behind. Pull the left-hand loop through to form an 'X' in the structure of the knot.

4. Where the two loops form an 'X' in front, reach up through each twisted loop with the left and right hand respectively.

5. Pull through each of the 'X' crosses with each hand to form the loops of the finished bowline. The standing parts uncross and lie parallel to each other.

6. Fair, and tighten the knot by pulling on both loops simultaneously with the standing parts.

Water Bowline

The Water Bowline improves holding on wet line and will not slide undone. In *ABOK* in 1944, Ashley did not name this knot, even though he published a diagram of how to tie it. However, Raoul Graumont did name it in his book, *Handbook of Knots* (1945), as well as in his *Encyclopedia of Fancy Knots and Ropework* written in conjunction with John Hensel (1942). The great value of the Water Bowline is that the added half hitch (referred to in old texts as a Cuckold Knot) prevents the loop around the underlying bight from becoming too tight, allowing the knot to be undone more readily and without affecting its security.

1. Form a regular Bowline Loop, with the standing part over the hand and a number 'six' on your palm.

2. Form a second identical overhand anticlockwise loop below the first and slide it up under the first loop.

3. Pass the working end up through both loops, just as you did for the regular bowline.

4. Take the working end around anti-clockwise behind the standing part, adjusting the length of the line to the desired size of your temporary loop.

5. Finish the loop knot by passing the working end down through the first and second loops, holding it to the right side of the formed loop before pulling on the standing part to tighten the knot. Push the second loop up to meet the first loop to enlarge the size of the finished loop.

Midshipman's Hitch

This example of a changeling hitch is rather remarkable. Forming an adjustable loop at the end of a line may be necessary when tightening a tent's guyline. Originally, the Midshipman's Hitch was used for stopping to another line, according to Luce and Lever, as early as 1819. However, Aldridge and Nicholls both show a Midshipman's Hitch as the alternative form of making the Blackwall Hitch for a hook, so evidently the purpose (or the name) has changed in the lifetime of the knot. Today, the Midshipman's Hitch is used to provide a loop knot that can be changed in size by slide-and-grip, to make a line tighter.

1. Pass the working end of the line in a round turn about the standing part of the line to which you are making the line fast.

2. Make a second turn, jamming the line between the first turn and the standing part.

3. Pass the working end for a third turn across the previous two, and bring it around the standing part.

4. Complete the hitch by passing the working end under its own part, forming a half hitch.

5. Fair the knot and work the turns down tight to the line.

6. Slide the knot away from the bight in the line, so as to tighten the hitch and the loop.

Overhand Loop

Readily formed yet difficult to untie because it tightens hard onto the trapped bight parts, the Overhand Loop may be formed in the bight or with a bight formed near the working end. Note that it may have to be cut out if a marlinespike or other knot-releasing tool is not at hand. Its value lies in the fact that there are no fancy turns or inversions, and that it may be formed while wearing gloves on a cold day!

1. Form a bight in the line where you require the loop and start to form an Overhand Knot (p30) with the bight.

2. Fair the knot and ensure that any crossed parts lie fair together.

Variation: Double Overhand Loop

1. Form a Double Overhand Knot (p30) using a bight in the line.

2. Fair up the knot and twist the parts together to form the loop.

3. Fair the knot and ensure that any crossed parts lie fair together.

Overhand Sliding Loop

We sometimes need a loop to clamp down onto an object; then again, sometimes we want to keep the loop open, but at the same time must be able to make the loop larger. This loop knot answers both needs, depending on how it is formed. The Overhand Sliding Loop formed in twine makes a handy loop to pass over the end of spectacles or sunglasses arms, where you can slide it closed as a keeper. When this knot is formed in line around the waist, a climber can use a Figure-of-Eight Knot (p34) as a stopper to hold the loop open around himself, thereby preventing the sliding feature.

1. Form a bight in the line large enough to pass over the object to be trapped, leaving enough length in the working end for the round turns and final knot.

2. Form an anti-clockwise overhand loop with the working end, by passing it around the standing part.

3. Loosely work the working end around the standing part, toward the bight, for the required number of turns, each laid alongside its predecessor.

4. Pass the working end down through the turns toward the standing part of the line and away from the bight.

5. Fair by carefully rotating the round turns around the standing part.

6. Tighten the knot by pulling on the non-sliding part and the working end. The loop may now be tightened down onto the object you wish to secure.

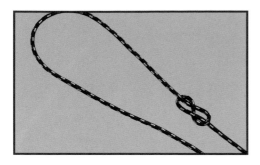

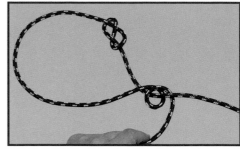

1. Tie a Figure-of-Eight Knot about 1m (1yd 3in) or so from the working end, to allow you enough line for the finishing knot.

2. Double the line to form a bight and pass it around your waist. Form an anticlockwise overhand loop by passing the working end around the standing part.

3. Repeat to form a second turn over the previous turn, with the working end toward your waist.

4. Tuck the working end down through the two round turns toward the standing part, and away from your waist.

5. Fair the knot down carefully to tighten it and make final adjustments in the position of the Figure-of-Eight Knot as required.

Figure-of-Eight Loop in the Bight

⚓ 🔺 ⌒ 🏠

Favoured heavily by firefighters, this loop knot is also an absolute must for climbers and anglers. It is very readily tied, maintains its security and can be untied if it has not been too heavily loaded. It is derived from the Figure-of-Eight Stopper Knot, but uses the bight with which the knot is made as a loop.

1. Form a bight of at least 250mm (10in or 20d) in the position required for the loop. Begin by passing the bight behind the standing part in an anticlockwise underhand loop.

2. Next, pass the bight in front of the standing part and again behind, ready to pass through the first loop formed.

3. Bring the bight up through the loop and fair the knot, ensuring that parallel parts do not cross over each other.

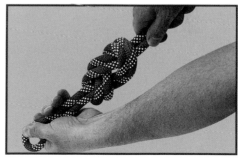

4. Tighten the loop by pulling in opposite directions on the standing parts and the bight.

Figure-of-Eight Loop
with Three Adjustable Loops

J | △ | ▲

Where a single loop in a Figure-of-Eight Knot is useful, three should be even better! This loop knot utilizes the power of the Figure-of-Eight Knot with a simple amendment to form a fan-anchor location or to form three positions for lures and leaders. The strength of this loop knot is that it absorbs load in three directions at once, while having self-adjusting loops that absorb the load and share it equally.

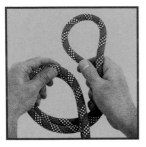

1. Form a bight of at least 250mm (10in or 20d). Pass the bight behind the standing part in an anticlockwise under-hand loop.

2. Next, pass the bight in front of the standing part and again behind, ready to pass through the first loop formed.

3. Bring the bight up through the loop. Fair, ensuring that parallel parts do not cross over each other. Extend the bight for the required length of all three bights.

4. Open the principal bight behind the parts of the bight. Tuck the end of the bight up into the top of the Figure-of-Eight Knot.

5. Pull the middle of the central bight up through the top and arrange the lengths of the legs according to your needs.

Tips

When extending the Figure-of-Eight Knot in Step 3, try rolling the paired parts simultaneously, to avoid possible tangling.

Threaded Figure-of-Eight Loop

Threading refers to the technique of retracing a knot back onto itself. The Threaded Figure-of-Eight Loop relies on doubling the figure of eight by refeeding the line. It can be very helpful when tied to a harness for safety, allowing the tyer to secure his harness to the end of the line. It is claimed by the caving authorities to be 80 per cent of the strength of the original line, a very strong knot indeed. The belayed climber can be reassured that this loop knot is reliable.

1. Pick a location about 1m (1yd 3in) back from the end of the line, and tie a Figure-of-Eight Knot (p34) at that point.

2. Pass the working end through your harness or the tie-off point and start following the standing part back into the knot.

3. Be sure to follow inside the line that exits the knot, so that the exiting line continues to remain on the outside of the finished knot.

4. Ensure that the parts lie parallel to each other, and that the working end has a tail of at least 20d.

5. Fair the knot so that all lines lie properly parallel, and then tighten the knot using both sides simultaneously.

Tips

Be sure to keep the end loop as short as possible, so that it does not snag on anything while in use.

Double Figure-of-Eight Loop

The unique features of this loop are that it allows for greater security, is stable and allows a climber to clip in two separately loaded carabiners without harm or foul. Known colloquially as 'Bunny-ears' to cavers, the Double Figure-of-Eight Loop may be used for a Y-belay, with one lead to the climber and one to the belay. It is a little bulkier than the Bowline in the Bight (p55), and is easier to tie and untie, so there are advantages to be had in learning how to tie this extended Figure-of-Eight Loop.

1. Make a bight in the line. Form an underhand anticlockwise loop with the bight end.

2. Bring the bight end over the standing part, as though beginning a Figure-of-Eight Loop in the Bight.

3. Pass the bight behind the first formed loop, but do not pull it through.

4. Reach up through the bight with the left hand and down into the first loop to grasp the two parts of the bight that lie behind the loop.

5. Pulling up on the bight parts, slip the bight off your wrist. Work bights out into loops. Ease the bight out and over the bulk of the Figure-of-Eight Knot so that it lies below the lowest turn of the doubled parts over the standing part.

6. Fair the knot, ensuring that the parts lie parallel and that the loops are of the required size. Tighten the knot by pulling on the standing parts and on the two loops.

Tips

It may seem difficult to tie, but if you persevere, you will find that this loop knot is easier to manage than the Bowline in the Bight.

double figure-of-eight loop   67

Hitches are used to secure a line to another object such as a ring, rope or rail and are used where that object plays no part in the structure of the hitch other than to form a base for it. Hitches attach at various angles, but they always provide a secure fixing. Possibly showing the greatest versatility and variability, hitches differ as a family from bends or knots in that they must develop friction with the object to which they are being tied. Hitches frequently require multiple turns around the object for this purpose. If frequent turns aren't possible, hitches use opposing turns over the line itself, thus increasing friction between the crossing parts of the line instead. A round turn distributes the load from the line directly to the object, provided the object itself is round. Angular objects tend to pinch the line and can produce kinking and overstressing. To avoid the stress caused by tying lines to, or across sharp edges, try spreading the load over stiff canvas or leather.

HITCHES

Anchor Bend

This is a hitch rather than a bend, but long usage has preserved its name. It is also known as the Fisherman's Bend from past work applications. Graumont and Hensel list variants of the Anchor Bend as having one half hitch or a seizing to finish. Its security is founded in the fact that it tightens onto itself, rather than onto the ring to which it is attached. This form of tightening allows the two parts of the line to rotate around the ring, rather than chafing it.

1. Make a full round turn around the ring or shackle with the working end. Now place one finger alongside the ring to make a gap and …

2. … pass the working end around the standing part, and through the gap when you withdraw your finger from the hitch, thus forming a half hitch around the round turn.

3. Bring the working end up parallel with the standing part, then pass it around the standing part and under itself to form a second half hitch.

4. Tighten the hitch down onto the ring or as close as needed. Fair the two half hitches together and draw tight.

Bachmann Knot

The Bachmann Knot is actually a hitch not a knot, because it is used to secure a line to a rope. It uses friction and a second object, a carabiner, to attach an ascender to an anchor line. Rather than relying on mechanical advantage, this hitch makes use of available equipment to gain resting friction during the ascension of a rope by a climber. Equally effective on wet and dry ropes, this hitch is a great favourite among climbers and mountaineers, although a few others also find a need for it.

1. Form a sling using the Double Fisherman's Knot (p110), preferably with 6mm (0.2in) cord. Slip the sling over a carabiner and hold the doubled sling against your ascending line.

2. Pass the doubled loop standing parts around the line, trapping the spine of the carabiner, four or five times depending on the degree of friction that you require.

3. To lock the carabiner in place, apply downward pressure toward the final pass while applying pressure to the sling of cord with the second carabiner.

4. To unlock the friction, push upward on the carabiner that is against the line to ease it away from the line. Now you can move the hitch further up the line.

Clove Hitch

Known also as the Dry Weather Hitch or Builder's Knot by Ashley, this most useful hitch appears in many guises and is known by different names. It forms the base for any number of other knots, bends and hitches, and is most useful when you need to restrain the working end on a knot. Used by sailors, climbers and campers, it may be tied in many different ways, one-handed or two-handed. When secured to a spar or pole the Clove Hitch has a tendency to work loose if it is subjected to rotation. Whenever it is used, try to ensure that both ends are loaded for greatest security. Try the variations to expand your repertoire and find your favourite.

Two-handed, with the Working End, on the middle of a Spar or Line

1. Pass a line over the spar, bringing it back up to one side of the standing part. Cross the working end diagonally in front of the standing part to form an 'X' on the spar.

2. Pass the working end around behind the spar again. Tuck it under the diagonal crossing part. You should now have two parallel parts and one diagonal crossing over both parallels.

3. Tighten by pulling on the working end and standing part simultaneously, to lock down the diagonal crossing part on the other two parts.

Tips

The working end may be passed to either side of the standing part – just remember to cross it over the standing part to the other side from which it started. Pull through a bight instead of the working end, so that the hitch is made slippery, for quick release.

Two-handed, in the Bight, on the end of a Spar or Bollard

1. Form an underhand anticlockwise loop where you need the hitch. Make the loop large enough to go around the spar or bollard.

2. Form a second loop, exactly like the first one, keeping it to one side.

3. Without twisting either loop, slide the first one under the second. Now you can see the crossing of the hitch nearest to you, with the parallel parts on the side of the hitch furthest from you.

Tips

Cross your hands in front of you. Grasp the line with each hand, and uncross your hands, still holding the line. If you started with your right hand nearest to you, put both loops on the right hand. Holding both parts in one hand, your Clove Hitch is ready to slip over the bollard!

Clove Hitch continued...

One-handed, Tying with a Bight on a Pole or Spar

1. Pass the line over the spar or pole, near the end, as a bight. The working end is nearest to you in this picture.

2. Reach behind the working part to grip the free part of the bight with your right hand, twisting it a half turn clockwise, so that the back of your hand is uppermost.

3. Continue to twist the free part clockwise, so that your hand now has the thumb uppermost. You have now formed an anticlockwise overhand loop.

4. Slip the loop over the end of the spar, trapping the standing parts together with the crossing diagonal. Tighten by pulling both standing parts.

Tips

The Clove Hitch and Cleat Hitch are the same structure. The latter has an extra turn around the base of the cleat with the standing part. Remember to look at the knot when finished to find two parallel lines, with one additional line diagonally trapping the two parallel lines.

One-handed, Tying with a Bight on a Carabiner

1. Unlock the gate of the carabiner and pass the line through so that the free part of the line is nearest to you, the working (loaded) part to your right.

2. Hold the left-most, free part of the line with your right hand, and the back of your hand facing you, thumb down.

3. Twist the right hand clockwise to form an anti-clockwise overhand loop.

4. Slip the new loop over the open carabiner, trapping the standing parts together with the crossing diagonal. Pull both of the standing parts to close the hitch and relock the gate.

Tips

If you only load one leg of this hitch, put a stopper on the other leg close to the diagonal crossing, or tie two half hitches around the loaded standing part, so that the free part does not pull through.

Boom Hitch

In *ABOK*, the Boom Hitch (#1687) is simply described as a decorative hitch with no other name. It is shown as a hitch finished with an Overhand Knot that can be pulled at right angles to the boom. Other authors such as Geoffrey Budworth, have found it useful for sheeting in any direction. My own trials on large and small round booms corroborate this opinion, but it does not work as well with squared section booms. A note of caution – never rely on this hitch as your means of attaching the main sheet to the boom if you do not know how to recreate it! This hitch is very good for eliminating costly fittings and can be used quickly and safely in conjunction with a couple of half hitches to hoist light spars, if done with care.

1. Pass the working end over the spar, bring it around the spar, and cross it over in front of the standing part.

2. Pass the working end over again, to cross at right angles to the previous pass.

3. Bring the working end behind the spar for a third time and cross it in front of the standing part, right to left. Finish to the left of all crossing turns.

4. Pass the working end behind for the fourth and last time, this time to the left of the standing part.

5. Cross the last pass (in front of the spar) with the working end. Now tuck the working end under the last previous pass to lock down the hitch. Pull on the standing part and the working end to fair the hitch.

Rigger's Hitch

This hitch is often mistaken for the Rolling Hitch, because both are formed in a similar way. However, the lock that is obtained with the Rigger's Hitch prevents it from moving or sliding along in either direction. Having learned this hitch from a master rigger, I in turn pass it on to upcoming knot-tyers. Since it is supposed to bend or kink the line to which it is applied, this hitch should be used sparingly on a spar or other solid object, but should perform much better when tied to another line.

1. Make a pass over the line to be hitched with the hitching line.

2. Make a round turn around the hitched line with the hitching line. The direction of pull here is to the left of the hitching line.

3. Make a second turn, but this time pass the hitching line up over the first turn, so that it crosses the first turn and passes to the right-hand side of the hitched line.

4. Finish round behind the standing part of the hitched line with a crossing pass, just like the last pass of a Clove Hitch (p72).

Tips

To free the hitching line more readily, form the final pass in Step 4 as a bight instead of passing the working end. Then you only have to pull the working end to free the hitch.

Rolling Hitch

The Rolling Hitch, sometimes previously referred to as Magnus or Magner's Hitch, is not to be confused with the Rigger's Hitch that appears similar in construction. The Rolling Hitch works well when formed in line that is smaller than the line that is hauled. Ashley states that this hitch (#1734) is used when bending to a spar, and, in an alternative form as the Rigger's Hitch (#1735), when bending to a line. The most common form found today is the one shown here, used mostly for bending to a line, with good grip.

1. Pass the hauling line across the standing part of the line to be hauled and make a round turn under its own standing part.

2. Make a second turn under the previous pass and cross the two parts diagonally, thereby trapping the two parts.

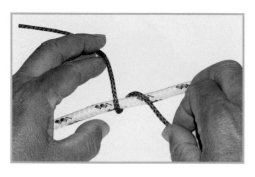

3. With turns to the right, pass the working end of the hauling line under its diagonal turn from left to right.

4. Fair the passes and tighten the hitch to complete. Pull downward to apply tension to the hauling line.

Buntline Hitch

⚓ ⚠ 🏠

The Buntline Hitch is one of those hitches that has survived from the days of square-rigged ships. Now it is used less for securing a line over the face of a sail to haul in the bunt, than to secure a line to a ring or around a small spar in such a way that it will not come off, even with a severe shaking. As such, it is useful to tie off a fly-sheet for a tent to a neighbouring anchor.

1. Pass the working end through from below the point of attachment.

2. Bring the working end across the standing part (left to right) and tuck it under the standing part (right to left), beginning the Clove Hitch around the standing part.

3. Cross the standing part once again with the working end, crossing the previous turn at a diagonal.

4. Tuck the working end under the standing part (again right to left), and make the final tuck under the diagonal crossing. Don't trap the first pass with this turn.

5. Draw the Clove Hitch tight, then pull the Clove Hitch down toward the ring or spar.

Cow Hitch

This hitch is also known as Lark's Head, Lanyard, Bale Sling, Ring, or Tag Hitch. It may have been called the Lark's Head, because the hitch looked a little like the head of a lark, or because it could be used to secure larks' feet when these were hunted for food. It is known as the Cow Hitch only in agricultural references where it is used to tie animals to a peg in the ground, and it is named the Lanyard Hitch when used in beading to secure the cord to a lanyard.

The Bale Sling Hitch name is used in seaports, where you also find it called a Ring Hitch, having been used both for slinging bales of cargo and for tying off to rings! As the Tag Hitch, it was used in tatting, the countryman's version of lace filigree made with one shuttle instead of dozens of bobbins. It can be tied with a working end or to a ring or spar in the bight, and so forms a useful addition to most knot-tying repertoires.

Tying with a Working End

1. Pass the working end through the ring to which the hitch is to be fixed and bring it to one side of the standing part.

2. Pass the working end in front of the standing part, then behind the ring or spar and through it from behind.

3. Tuck the working end down through the crossing part, parallel with the standing part. Pull both parts down and away to tighten.

Tying with a Bight: Lark's Head

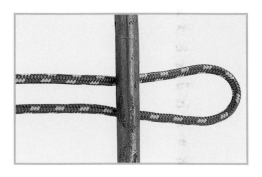

1. Form a bight in the line and pass it up and behind the spar.

2. Open the bight out and bring it over the front of the spar. Now pull both ends through the bight.

3. Pull on both ends to tighten the knot.

Tips

This hitch is so versatile, you should experiment with it to find the best use for yourself. I have used it to tie to a kite's bridle, to secure a jib down to the foredeck, to secure a continuous sheet to the jib clew and to form part of a magic trick for children.

Pedigree Cow Hitch

Though the name of this hitch suggests that it is intended for but one purpose, don't let that stop you from trying it out in different situations. Its value is that it is unlikely to come off when it is rotated around a post if only one end is attached to the cow. It also tightens no matter which way it is pulled, so beware! The pull on this hitch may be at any angle. I have used it to hang brooms by the handle – this hitch on the handle and the other end of the line passed through a drilled batten with a stopper knot.

1. Form a Cow Hitch (p80) and select the shorter of the two parts as the working end.

2. Tuck the short working end between the ring and the bight.

3. Tighten the working end to secure the hitch.

Tips

To untie this handy hitch, push the bight away from the ring with your thumb to loosen the hold on the standing part. This action works the standing part loose to enable the tucked working end to be freed.

Figure-of-Eight Hitch

Icons: ⚔ △ J ⌂

This easy-to-tie hitch can be used in many ways. Climbers use it for securing a coil's hanging loop to the harness loop, sailors use it to start a fixing to a spar, anglers use it to secure leaders through their loops, and it has many other applications. The security of the hitch derives from the fact that the working end twists back on itself, thus trapping it against the spar or ring. Use a line that is smaller than the spar or ring to which the hitch is attached to allow as much spreading of the load as possible. In rotational applications, this hitch does not work as well, so use it judiciously. Load should be applied only at right angles to the hitch.

1. Pass the line over the spar or ring base and bring the working end up on the side of the standing part.

2. Bring the working end across the standing part and tuck it behind the standing part to start a Figure-of-Eight Knot (p34). Complete the Figure-of-Eight Knot by passing the working end up toward the base and tucking it between the formed loop and the base. Leave about 12d of line beyond the hitch.

3. Now pull on the standing part to tighten the hitch.

Tips

For greater security, add your favourite stopper knot to the working end after forming the hitch.

French Prusik

This hitch is believed to have been invented in the late 1970s by a French climber named Machard. It was then known in France as the Machard Tresse, but has since become known in the English-speaking world as the French Prusik. However, the hitch is shown in a 1917 edition of *Bluejacket's Manual of the United States Navy* and marked as a 'Strop on a Rope'

for hooking a tackle, so it may not be that new. The hitch is found useful by some as an abseiling (rappelling) aid. Because it can be released under load, however, you should use it with great caution and only after extensive training. Simple to tie, the French Prusik requires the use of a carabiner here, but may also be used with other tie-offs.

1. Form a cord sling using a Double Fisherman's Knot (p110) and pass the sling around the anchor line with one round turn.

2. Continue passing the knotted end around the line for a total of three or more round turns.

3. Bring the knotted part of the sling down to meet the first part of the sling, so that you can pass a carabiner through both.

4. Tighten the hitch by applying tension downward until it kinks the anchor line. Applying pressure to the upper turns of the hitch may result in it moving downward. This allows the hitch to slide into the required location.

Extended French Prusik

Invented by forensic knot specialist Robert Chisnall in the early 1980s, this knot enables the use of narrow webbing or tape, without having to tie a loop. The principle of this hitch is that it can maintain friction while retaining the ability to release that friction whenever needed and move to the desired location. It slides until it can gain enough friction with the anchor line(s) when formed in webbing, and locks in place by applying a slight kink to the line(s), while gripping the anchor line.

1. Tie an Overhand Loop (p60) in each end of a length of webbing. Allow at least 600mm (24in) for 11mm (0.4in) line with three wraps. Beginning at the centre of the length of the webbing, wrap it around the anchor line.

2. Make alternating wraps around the line, keeping the intermediate diamond shapes between successive crossings as small as possible.

3. As you continue wrapping, ensure that you oppose the direction of the previous turn. If you have wrapped the previous turn over-under, make the next one under-over on the same side of the line.

4. Pass the open carabiner through the opposed overhand loops that will suspend the load. The loops should be as close as possible to the line, so make more turns if needed.

Gaff Topsail Halyard Bend

The gaff topsail is a sail that extends fore and aft on a schooner-rigged ship, extending from the top of the foremast or mainmast down to meet the gaff of the foresail or mainsail respectively. The older forms of the gaff topsail had a trapezoid shape, fitted with a gaff spar at the head of the sail for raising, and meeting the gaff of the mainsail at the foot of the topsail. Later versions did away with this refinement, and replaced the trapezoidal gaff topsail with a simpler triangular shape, having no separate topsail gaff. This secure hitch was the means for raising and keeping in place that gaff, which was bent on and swayed up when the sail was set in light winds. Today, the hitch can also be secured to a spar or ring, as a quick and easy hitch.

1. Pass the working end over the spar from behind.

2. Make a full, round turn-and-a-half to one side of the standing part.

3. Check which side the turn was made (Step 2) and pass the working end behind the standing part from the same side.

4. Bring the working end across and tuck it beneath the round turn to complete the hitch snugly against the spar.

5. Fair the hitch by pulling on the standing part to tighten, ensuring that the round turn parts lie close against each other.

Tips

If this hitch rotates, it may come loose. To prevent this, tie your favourite stopper knot in the working end.

Heddon Knot

⚓ 🔺 🔼 🏠

According to Geoffrey Budworth, Chet Heddon invented this hitch in 1959. First appearing in *Summit Magazine* in 1960, it was subsequently named the Kreuzklem in 1964. It is also known to climbers as the Cross-Prusik Knot. Both names identify something more about the structure of the hitch than is indicated by its inventor's name. *Kreuzklemm* means 'cross clamp' and so gives an indication of what the hitch is used for and how it is made. A Prusik wraps around the base line as does this hitch, hence the similarity. Initially used by climbers for safety, this hitch is being used more extensively by riggers and those who work aloft on ships as a means of ensuring a safe belay to their anchor line.

1. Form a sling from cord or webbing about 300mm (12in) in length between each bight. Bring one bight behind the anchor line and back to the front of the line.

2. Cross the other part of the sling over the first bight, trapping it over itself.

3. Make a second crossing the sling, trapping against the anchor line. Then tuck the longer end of the sling through the short bight and tighten the hitch down so that the bight rests against the anchor line.

4. Apply downward pressure to the free end of the sling to activate the hitch and release it to slide the sling up or down the anchor line.

Highwayman's Hitch

Also known as a Draw Hitch because of the draw loop inserted as the final tuck, this hitch works well to hold the load applied to the standing part. The hitch draws together well and remains tight, despite tugging on the standing part. For that reason alone, it works well to temporarily restrain a dinghy riding at a dock. The working end, if left sufficiently long and draped into the bow of the dinghy, can be pulled from inside the dinghy. The entire hitch will come loose into the dinghy and you will not have to feed any turns out through the ring or hitching rail.

1. Bring a bight of the line behind the rail or the ring.

2. Using the standing part of the line, or the end attached as a painter to the bow of the dinghy, bring a second bight up from the front and insert it from front to back into the first bight. Tighten the first bight.

3. Using the working end, form a third bight and pass it into the second bight. Tighten the second bight down onto the third, by pulling on the standing part.

Tips

For additional security, pass a fourth bight on the working end into the third bight. Adjustment will then have to be made by working the working end around inside its own bight.

Klemheist Knot

Similar to the French Prusik and Extended French Prusik, the Klemheist is another favourite among climbers and mountaineers. Despite preferences for one system or other, this hitch has certainly received support from the majority of climbers I have talked to. The structure combines friction in the riding turns with a passed bight to lock around the round turns. Made with a sling of cord, it is one of those self-rescue hitches with which many a climber has been helped to safety, while hanging on with one hand.

1. Form a sling in 6mm (0.2in) accessory cord with a Double Fisherman's Knot (p110). Wrap the sling around the base line on which support is required, using the bight, not the knotted portion.

2. Make three turns and pass the bight away from the knotted part.

3. Turn the bight down toward the knotted part of the sling and pass the knotted part through the bight from inside to outside.

Tips

Greater handling grip can be afforded if you insert a carabiner between the round turns and the base line.

Lighterman's Hitch

⚓ ⛺ 🏠

Also known as a Tugboat Hitch in California, and as a Mooring Hitch by author Gordon Perry, this hitch allows a loaded line to be transferred to a Samson post or winch and then to be secured while still under load. According to Geoffrey Budworth, this hitch was used by Thames lightermen to secure their surging loads alongside the docks and vessels from which they loaded their cargos. Ashley calls the hitch a Backhanded Mooring Hitch (#1795). No matter what the name, the hitch is extremely useful for attaching a line under load to a post so that the load can be gradually released or applied under tension.

1. Make a clockwise round turn of the line around a post. Take two or three turns, depending on the load that you want to support.

2. Form and pass a bight of the line anticlockwise under the loaded standing part, keeping the working end on the same side. Shown here, the bight is being passed over the standing part, prior to passing it under the standing part, with the working end trapped in the hand.

3. Pass the bight formed over the top of the post. Draw it tight with the working end.

Tips

Be sure to fair each succeeding turn tightly (make each turn fast) before proceeding, so that the hitch does not release slowly. Be sure not to stand in line with a loaded line.

4. Take the working end and pass it clockwise around the post in a half turn.

5. When necessary, repeat the passing of a bight and then a half turn around the standing part. Finish with a half hitch over the standing part.

Mooring Hitch

Referred to as a High Post Hitch (#1809) by Ashley, this hitch provides a useful addition to the knot-tyer's repertoire. To add confusion to the naming of knots and hitches, however, Ashley's own Mooring Hitch (#1791) is nothing like this one. The essential difference is that this Mooring Hitch allows the line to be retrieved from the vessel without one having to be on the dock when releasing it, an important consideration with a large tidal range. The line remains around the post, however. Use the Highwayman's Hitch (p88) for complete retrieval.

1. Pass the working end around the hitching post. Bring the working end forward toward the front of the standing part.

2. Form the shape of an underhand clockwise loop in the working end and pass it over the standing part, leaving the working end long.

3. Form a bight in the remaining working end. Weave the bight over and under the underhand clockwise loop, starting on the right, over the loop's crossing parts, behind the standing part, and finally over the left part of the loop. Pull on the bight to tighten the loop onto the bight.

Tips

When a small boat's painter is secured mooring to a quayside ring or to a piling ring, slide and relock the Hitch to meet the changing tide level.

Munter Friction Hitch

The Backhanded Hitch by Ashley (#1851) is a Munter Friction Hitch with stopping added. As the Italian Hitch or Sliding Ring Hitch, the Munter Friction Hitch is recognized by the Union Internationale des Associations d'Alpinisme (UIAA) as a means of belaying an alpine climber, but is not the official method of belay, particularly for sport climbing where there have been many recorded falls. Pit Schubert, President of the Safety Commission of the UIAA, has said that this is a braking sling, not a knot or hitch, because it moves under load. It is known in German as the Halbmastwurfsicherung or HMS for short. By applying pressure to the inactive part of the line, this hitch effectively stops movement of the line through the carabiner. The hitch may also be used in abseiling down a line but tends to twist or kink and destroy the line by burning the cover or sheath.

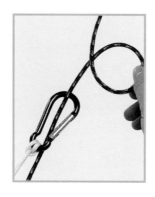

1. Pass the line from the active part (the part that is connected to the climber's harness, which would here be in the upper right of the picture) over and down into the gate of the carabiner. The carabiner should already be attached with a sling of webbing to a suitable anchor (here in the lower left).

2. Grip the active part and twist it so that you form the overhand clockwise loop shown here. Grip the line with the back of your hand toward you, and then turn your hand so that the palm faces you.

3. Pass the loop over the bill of the carabiner, trapping the loop against itself. Close the carabiner gate properly.

4. Close the gate and apply pressure to the inactive part to temporarily hold the line (shown here to the lower left, for a belay from above). Belay from below by passing the inactive line down to the lower level and applying tension in the direction of the climber (upper right). See Munter Mule (p94) for a method of locking the Hitch.

Tips

Never rely on a hitch as your sole means of belay and do not practise abseiling without extensive training.

Marlinespike Hitch

Use this handy hitch to pull on a line or twine whenever you need additional leverage. Pulling on the twine directly may cut into your hands. The marlinespike itself may be found on some folding rigging knives or as a separate tool supplied with a sheath-type rigging knife. It is a tapered steel spike that is usually polished and has a blunt duck bill- shaped tip. The hitch readily collapses when the marlinespike is removed, so that the twine is not compromised.

1. Form an Overhand Knot with a Draw Loop (Slippery Overhand Knot, p31) in the line that is to be pulled tight.

2. When you insert a marlinespike pull the loop tight around it. Now pull on the marlinespike at right angles to the twine, pulling the twine from right to left.

Munter Mule

The Munter Hitch really needs a locking structure to be of more complete assistance. The Munter Mule ensures that the Munter Hitch (and many other hitches) will not come undone at unexpected moments. As a safety hitch, it frees both hands when you are conducting a rescue of a person on belay, thus becoming one of a panoply of backup knots and hitches that are essential knowledge for the competent knot-tyer. It is known as a mule because it can support a great load!

1. First form the Munter Friction Hitch as shown on p92.

2. Then form an underhand loop in the inactive part of the line, passing the standing part of that line in a clockwise direction under itself.

3. In the working end of the inactive part, form a long bight. Pass this bight over the standing part of the active part of the line and down into the small loop formed in Step 2. Fair and tighten this part of the hitch.

4. Tie an Overhand Knot (p30) around the active line and then tighten it down.

5. Repeat the passing of a bight and then a half turn around the standing part until the line is used. Finish with a half hitch over the standing part.

Tips

If you intend the knot to be shockloaded, do not over tighten in Steps 4 and 5 above.

Ossel Hitch

The word 'ossel' appears neither in the *Encyclopedia Britannica* nor in the *Compact Oxford English Dictionary*. It does appear in Geoffrey Budworth's *Ultimate Encyclopedia of Knots* and in the *Encyclopedia of Knots and Fancy Rope Work* by Graumont & Hensel. Apparently an 'ossel' is a Scottish gill net, now banned. The hitch is an elegant, simple method of attaching one pendant line to another and does not come undone when rotated.

1. Pass the working end over from behind the base line and bring it to the front of the line, taken here to the left.

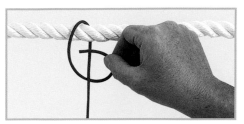

2. Work the working end behind the standing part, bringing it back in front of the base line and forming a bight around the back of the standing part.

3. Pass the working end over the base line again, but from front to back instead, on the opposite side from the first pass.

4. Bring the working end across the standing part again and tuck it down into the bight formed in Step 2. Pull the working end through 12d.

5. Fair the knot by pulling on the standing part and pushing upward on the hitch.

Palomar Knot

J △

Lefty Kreh and Mark Sosin in their book *Practical Fishing Knots* (1972) rated the strength of common fishing knots based on their own experiences. They rate the Palomar Knot at between 95 and 100 per cent of the breaking strength of the line. When tied in perfect monofilament, this is probably true but misleading, because it so rarely occurs. This hitch, tied in the bight, is unlikely to slip or collapse. It can be readily applied to a loop on a fishing hook or to the staple of your pocketknife.

1. Pass a bight of the line up through the ring or closed loop to which the hitch is to be tied.

2. Cross the bight in front of the standing part to form an Overhand Knot (p30).

3. Open the bight and pass the ring or the hook end through the opened bight.

4. Bring the opened bight down behind the standing parts to rest against them.

5. Fair the hitch and tighten by pulling on the standing part, easing the Overhand Knot around the standing part.

Tips

When tied in non-monofilament line, the hitch can be difficult to tighten. Try pulling the Overhand Knot two parts at a time from the bight through to its passage around the ring.

Pile Hitch/Double Pile Hitch

⚓ 🔺 🏠

This hitch has been used for securing ships to mooring piles for many years, because it is easy to attach and detach. It is also very secure when pulled from almost any angle. Its security exceeds that of the Clove Hitch (p72) because it does not matter whether it rotates around the pile or whether the pull on the pile is upward or downward. It holds tight under just about any circumstances.

1. Form a bight in the line and pass it around the pile to which it is to be hitched.

2. Bring the bight around below the standing part in a round turn.

3. Continue to bring the bight up from below the standing part and open it enough so that it can be passed over the top of the pile.

4. After opening the bight, pass it over the top of the pile across the standing parts, then tighten down the hitch.

Tips

To make a Double Pile Hitch, make a further turn around the pile after Step 2. To open the hitch, move one part of the bight sharply away from the pile, moving the standing parts to give slack to the hitch and allow the bight to be released from the top.

Trucker's Hitch

Also known as the Wagoner's Hitch, this popular hitch is often mistied, perhaps because it seems too easy to tie or because people fear it will come undone unless there is some gigantic knot in the line. Rated at 2:1, the purchase power of the hitch increases the ability of the tyer to make the line exceptionally tight when used on a load. It is frequently used to secure a load in the back or to the roof of vehicles. The friction in the hitch ensures that it stays secure, yet is easily released when tension is taken off the line.

1. Start tying a Round Turn and Two Half Hitches (p100) on one side of the vehicle, then pass the line over the load.

2. Form an overhand anti-clockwise loop in the line at least 600mm (24in) away from the attaching point.

3. In the remaining line, form a bight around 150mm (5.85in) in length. Form a second bight in the end of the first bight.

Tips

Because this hitch relies on tension to keep it in place, and also to prevent vibration from undoing it, it is wise to pass a toggle through the second bight (formed in Step 4) prior to tightening.

4. Insert the second bight into the loop formed in Step 2. Twist the large bight to trap the second bight in the loop.

5. Now continue by twisting the large bight anticlockwise. Consequently, the loop remains in place from the effect of these twists.

6. Form a third bight in the working end of the line, pulling it down through the twisted bight. This will be moved to the anchor position.

7. Maintain tension as you slip the third bight over the anchor piece or hook.

8. Pull on the working end to maintain the tension. Finish with two half hitches around the lowest parts of the hitch.

9. Subsequent hitches may be formed adjacent to the first if needed.

Round Turn and Two Half Hitches

This hitch is a personal favourite because of its ability to hold well under almost any condition. Applying a seizing between the working end and the standing part of the hitch after it is formed guarantees that this remarkable hitch will not let go until it reaches about 90 per cent of the strength of the line. The strength in tension of this hitch derives from the fact that the line makes a round turn about the spar before being hitched to itself, but without bending the strained line. Typically, knots, bends and hitches form weakened areas in the line due to compression of the fibres in a concentrated pinch point, which this hitch avoids handsomely.

1. Pass the working end around your chosen object, to make a complete round turn. Be sure not to trap the line under itself.

2. Form a half hitch over the standing part of the line, close to the round turn. Passed from left to right, it must be faired tight to the spar.

3. Form a second half hitch, passing the working end in the same direction, so as to form a Clove Hitch (p72) on the standing part.

Timber and Killick Hitch

The 18th-century word 'killick' or 'killock' refers to a stone or other heavy object to which a line was tied, for use as an anchor by a dinghy or other small craft. It is also used to refer to the Leading Seaman rank in a mess on board ship, whose badge shows a navy anchor. The Timber Hitch was used then as now to haul logs from the felling to the loading area of a dray for processing into lumber. The Timber Hitch forms the first part of the Killick Hitch and is still used today in logging practices.

1. Form a pass with the working end over the object to be hitched.

2 Bring the working end around and over the standing part in an elbow in order to trap the standing part.

3. Pass the working end under the round turn part at least three times, depending on the size of the object.

4. Pulling on the standing part causes the hitch to tighten and allows the twists around the line to tighten against the object. This forms the Timber Hitch.

5. To form the Killick Hitch, add a half hitch a distance away from the Timber Hitch, depending on the length of the object.

Tips

This hitch works well to form a tie for the attaching end of a jiffy reefing line around the boom of a sailboat if the original line has parted.

Bends join two pieces of line to lengthen the principal line or to form another strong structure. The strength of the bend depends on the number of pinch points, also known as nips, which remain in the structure. More pinch points weaken the line, but certainly forming a bend is much faster than forming a splice.

Several authors have shared their obvious delight in showing the symmetry and utility of bends by detailing them in their books, for instance in Charles Warner's *A Fresh Approach to Knotting and Ropework*, in Roger Miles' *Symmetric Bends,* and of course in *ABOK*, Chapter 18. We are reminded in maritime situations that 'bends are our friends' because they are tied and untied so readily. The bends detailed in this chapter may be tied in the ends of rope, twine, flat tape, and slick monofilament, or in a combination of these materials.

BENDS

Hunter's Bend

In the same year that Keith Moon of The Who, Pope Paul VI and Pope John Paul died within 30 days of each other, compact discs were invented and the first test tube baby was born, another amazing controversy hit the front pages of *The Times* of London. In 1978, Dr Edward Hunter claimed the Hunter's Bend as a new invention, but it was later shown to have been published in 1950 by Phil Smith as a Rigger's Knot. This controversy stirred the otherwise reticent knotters around Great Britain to form, in 1982, the International Guild of Knot Tyers. The bend itself is most useful for joining slippery line, such as polypropylene, and can readily be untied.

1. Lay two lines adjacent to each other so that they overlap their working ends by around 300mm (12in).

2. Form an overhand clockwise loop, using the doubled working ends. Take care that you keep the parts parallel.

3. Use the left-most working end and pass it up into the centre of the doubled loop.

4. Use the right-most working end and pass it down into centre of the doubled loop.

5. Holding the two working ends, proceed to fair the knot by pulling on the two standing parts, until the shape in the photo appears. When viewed from behind, the bend shows two diagonally-aligned parts.

Ashley's Bend

A guru of knot-tying, author Clifford Ashley produced details of several original knots, among them *ABOK* #1452. This bend was later named in his honour by Cyrus Day, another highly respected knot-tyer. The International Guild of Knot Tyers in the USA once tried to get the US Post Office to depict this bend for a postage stamp. The bend is so useful that they were convinced Ashley's name would thus be memorialized. The USPS has not yet accepted the stamp as of the writing of this book. Nevertheless, it is still a most useful bend for tying shock cord or other elastic material.

1. Form an underhand loop clockwise with one end of a line using the left hand. The working end is to the left in this photo.

2. Insert the standing part of the second line under the first loop from four o'clock. Bring enough through to make another underhand loop clockwise. Here the working end of the second line is parallel to the first working end, and over the standing part of the first line.

3. Hold both working ends together and pass them down and through the two underhand loops, so that they exit at one o'clock. Pull them firmly.

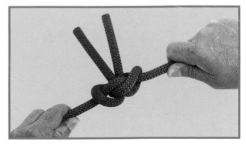

4. Fair the knot by pulling on both standing parts in opposing directions, so that the working ends appear on one side of the bend together.

Sheet Bend

Used when tying two lines of different diameter together, the Sheet Bend ranks very high among bends for everyday use and it is taught as one of the staples of modern knot-tying. Whether it is used to tie an extension to a weaving or knitting yarn, or to haul a hawser from a large vessel to the shore, the bend should be tied with both line ends on one side of the knot or it may open unexpectedly. Cyrus Day's experiments in 1935 revealed that when tied with the ends on opposing sides of the bend, the knot gave way more readily. You have been warned!

1. Form a bight in the thicker of the two lines that you are going to bend together. Bring the working end of this line to one side.

2. Bring the smaller of the two lines up through the bight, passing it to the same side as the bight's working end.

3. Bring the small line around behind the bight, leaving it a little proud of the bight.

4. Pass the small line over and across the bight, tucking it under itself where it exits from the bight.

5. Fair the knot by pulling down on the standing part of the small line to tighten and hold the bight parts together, and nipping the small line onto itself.

Double Sheet Bend

The utility of the Sheet Bend is only exceeded by its counterpart, the Double Sheet Bend. More secure and just as easy to tie and untie, the Double is a most handsome bend. Use it wherever security is of paramount importance: when towing, securing a small line to an exceptionally thick line, or when the larger of two lines is very stiff and cannot be bent into anything more than a bight.

1. Form a bight in the thicker of the two lines to be bent together. Bring the working end of this line to one side of the knot, shown here on the right.

2. Bring the smaller of the two lines up through the bight, passing it to the same side as the working end of the bight.

3. Bring the small line around behind the bight, leaving it slightly proud of the bight. Tuck the small line behind itself over the bight of the thicker line.

4. Pass the small line under behind the bight a second time, tucking it under itself once more alongside its previous path.

5. Fair the knot by pulling down on the standing part of the small line to tighten and hold the bight parts together, and nipping the small line onto itself. You will also need to tug the working end of the small line, to fair both turns of the doubling.

Tucked Sheet Bend

⚓ 🔺 ∪ 🏠

The slipped or draw loop has been mentioned several times in this book, but the practice of tucking the working end has not yet been addressed. The Tucked Sheet or One-Way Sheet Bend is the first of this type of structure mentioned here. The working end is tucked, in this case in line with the bend, to stop it from accidentally dislodging. When towing a vehicle, or when dragging the bend across the ground repeatedly, this handy tuck will prevent the working end from snagging on rocks or twigs, and the bend from being forced open.

1. Form a bight in the thicker of the two lines to be bent together. Bring the working end of this line to one side of the knot.

2. Bring the smaller of the two lines up through the bight, passing it to the same side as the working end of the bight.

3. Bring the small line around behind the bight, leaving the small line slightly proud of the bight.

4. Tuck the smaller of the two lines behind itself, but over the bight of the thicker line.

5. Bring the working end of the small line back on itself, tucking it under itself once more, alongside the bight working end.

5. The half-hitch should now be snugged against all the bight parts.

Fisherman's Knot

Inconsistent naming caused this bend to become known as a knot (the Fisherman's Bend is quite different and is actually a hitch!). Used by fishermen all over the world, the Fisherman's Knot joins two pieces of line of the same thickness so as to extend the length of a shorter line. It is variously listed in *ABOK* as the Waterman's Knot,

Water Knot, True Lover's Knot, Englishman's Knot and English Knot. This bend should not be used to join large-diameter lines together, because the line is difficult to fair into a secure knot. Further, when made in slippery line, the knot can readily come apart after only a few pulls.

1. Lay the working ends of the two lines beside each other to overlap by about 40d. Form an Overhand Knot (p30) with one working end by passing it around the standing part of the second line, then finishing the Overhand Knot along the standing part.

2. Reverse the lines on your working surface. Repeat the procedures in Step 1 with the other working end.

3. Draw the two standing parts apart so that the Overhand Knots slide toward each other and nest together for a secure fit. Fair the knot.

Double Fisherman's Knot

The need for greater security with the popular Fisherman's Knot brought about this variation, the Double Fisherman's Knot, which works just as well with fishing line as it does with 5mm (0.2in) low-stretch, high tensile strength cords for slinging anchors. This allows two lines to be tied securely, even in larger sized line. It is known to fishermen as the Grinner Knot, and to climbers as the Grapevine Knot or Double English Knot, an essential part of their repertoire. So many names, but one purpose – to bend two lines together! Cut the working end off at about 2d so that the knot can move through rod guides, but leave a working end of at least 12d if used for anchor slinging.

1. Lay the two lines beside each other, overlapping by about 350mm (13.7in). Using the working end of the left line, bring it behind the standing part and tie a Double Overhand Knot (p30) around the second line.

2. Reverse the two lines and repeat the procedure from Step 1, so forming a second Double Overhand Knot. If you cannot reverse the lines, tie the knot anticlockwise.

3. Slide the two knots together, so that they mate and match. Fair the knot to complete.

Triple Fisherman's Knot

If one knot is good and two are better, why not three? It was likely the invention of Spectra, a notoriously slippery and very strong line, that brought about the need for this extension of the Fisherman's Knot. Also known as a Double Grinner Knot by fishermen, it works well with slippery and wet monofilaments. Climbers use it to ensure security in Spectra cords and when the line or cord is used in wet conditions.

1. Tie a Triple Overhand Knot (p30) around one of the standing parts. This knot passes clockwise around the standing part when viewed from the standing part of the tying line.

2. Repeat Step 1 using the other end, either by reversing the lines or by tying anticlockwise toward the working end.

3. Draw the two knots together, fairing them as you do to ensure a good lock.

Double Carrick Bend – Ends Adjacent

Used as an heraldic device by Hereward the Wake since AD1070, the Double Carrick Bend is also known as the Josephine Knot by needle workers, but is unknown to most sailors. It reduces the tensile strength of the line by about 45 per cent, which is not as good as a single Bowline, but better than the Sheet Bend and the Reef Knot. When tying the knot, try this method of weaving the lines to end up with a stout bend, useful wherever you want to secure two lines of the same thickness together.

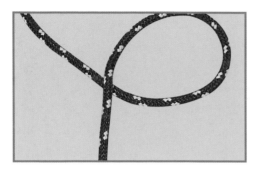

1. Form an overhand loop in the first line, anticlockwise, so that the working end finishes at about the six o'clock position.

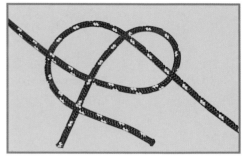

2. Lay the second line from right to left across the loop parts, parallel to the first standing part. Tuck the second working end under the first standing part. Now pass the second working end over the first.

3. Pass the second working end under the first loop, over its own standing part, and finally under the last part of the first loop. Both working ends are now on opposite sides of the knot.

4. Holding the two working ends, pull together on the standing parts, then pull the two standing parts apart to form the finished bend. The two working ends end up lying together on the same side of the bend.

Double Carrick Bend – Ends Opposed

1. Form an overhand loop in the first line, clockwise, so that the working end finishes at about the four o'clock position.

2. Bring the second line under the first loop from left to right, parallel to the first working end. Pass the second working end over the first working end, and then tuck it under the first standing part.

3. Weave the second working end over the first loop, under its own standing part and finally over the last part of the first loop. Both working ends are now on the same side of the knot.

4. Fair the knot, but remember that this is decorative, so do not pull the knot too tight.

Tips

The more decorative uses of this knot require that it be left unfaired. When doing this, try making the knot with two or more passes so that the line will lie flat.

Albright Special

Fishermen will frequently encounter the need to tie thicker or heavier test line to a finer one, and the Albright Special fits the bill perfectly. Similar to the Sheet Bend (p106) in that it bends a thin line to a thick one, the Albright Special can be used with wire leaders as well as monofilament to produce a bend that flies through rod guides for easier casting. Wetting the turns of the bend, prior to trimming it, assists in getting the bend as tight as possible.

1. Make a bight in the heavier line, about 5–7cm (2–3in) in length. Use a small piece of tape to hold the working end to the standing part.

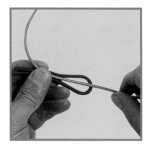

2. Lay about 10cm (4in) of the smaller line on top of the bight with the working end toward the open end of the bight. Hold in place with your left hand.

3. Wrap the smaller leader line around itself and the bight, making the turns tight as you go, and working toward the closed end of the bight.

4. Wrap the leader around at least six times being sure to trap it all the way on the same side of the parts of the bight.

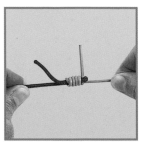

5. Tuck the working end of the leader through the bight. Pull steadily on the standing part of the leader, wetting the turns as needed to reduce friction. Pull the working end of the leader into the bight and cut away excess working ends.

Blood Knot

Also known as a Barrel Knot, the Blood Knot can be used wherever there is a need to join two ends or pieces of line securely. The knot is impossible to undo when tightened. Many fishermen tying this knot in monofilament will moisten it before tightening to ease the turns into place securely.

1. Lay the two ends of line side by side to form an overlap of at least 40d. This length will allow you to make at least six turns for joining slippery line.

2. Pass the left-hand working end around the second line, toward yourself, so that you form one turn over the standing parts of both lines.

3. Make the five or six round turns over the standing part, then tuck the working end of the first line between the two lines and hold it there with the fingers of your left hand.

4. Repeat Steps 2 and 3, using the working end from the second line. If you turned the first working end towards you, turn this working end away from you.

5. Complete the same number of turns as for the first working end. Tuck the working end of your second line in opposite direction to the first working end.

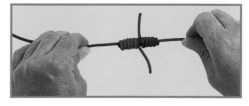

6. Finally, to fair the knot, pull both standing parts away from each other so that the working ends are held firmly in the centre of the formed knot.

Double Harness Bend – Parallel Ends

Also known as a Drawing Bend or Parcel Bend, the Double Harness Bend is used wherever you wish to tie two lines together, with either one of them under strain. Typical applications for the Double Harness Bend are to tie broken horse tack and broken shoelaces. It can also be used for tying packages, or for tying nylon webbing straps together. This bend is particularly good with twines and cords. The speed with which a professional packer can tie this knot is quite amazing.

1. Carefully form a clockwise underhand loop in the line under tension, taking the working end down (to the left here). Holding the crossing of the loop, bring the second working end up through the loop then down over the left leg of the loop, to finish under the first line's working end.

2. Pull the working end up between the loop and the second line to hold the strained line under tension. The photo shows this apart for the sake of clarity.

3. Hold the first working end and second standing part crossing. Bring the second line's working end under the standing part of the first line and wind it over the standing part to finish on the left side of the standing part. Note the 'mouth' through which the first working end appears.

4. Pass the second working end under its standing part, and enter the 'mouth' from below, to parallel the first working end.

Double Overhand Bend

Ashley refers to it as the Ring or Gut Knot, but this bend is also known as a Tape Knot or as a variety of Water Knot, and in the past was sometimes called a Regular Overhand Bend. It allows two lines to be brought together securely, particularly when using webbing (tape) or cords. It is most secure in wet conditions and is regularly used for webbing slings in climbing.

1. Form an Overhand Knot (p30) in one piece of line. Leave the knot loose.

2. Pass the other line or webbing in the opposite direction. Starting from the working end of the first piece, pass the second working end along the same path formed by the first knot.

3. Trace the entire knot with the second working end, pulling it through as needed. This will readily be seen when tying webbing. Leave the second working end sticking out as much as the first working end.

4. Fair the knot by holding each working end against the standing part and pulling in opposite directions. If using cords or rope, be sure that the lines do not cross each other in their paths.

Flemish Bend

Also known as the Figure-of-Eight Bend or Flemish Knot, this bend is favoured by climbers. Easily tied and secure, it differs from the Double Figure-of-Eight Bend in that it allows one line to follow the other, rather than having two separate knots joined into a bend. 'Flemishing' is a term used by sailors of old to denote the action of following or pairing lines adjacent to each other, after Flemish naval practices.

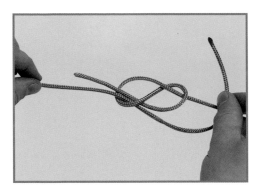

1. Form a Figure-of-Eight Knot (p34) in the end of one line. Leave a tail of about 150mm (6in) or so.

2. Pass the working end of the second line parallel to the first working end, in the opposite direction, so that it 'follows' the previous knot.

3. Trace around the first Figure-of-Eight Knot with the second working end, emerging alongside the first standing part.

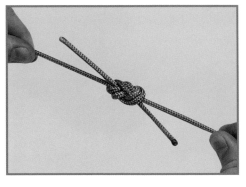

4. Holding the working ends and standing parts together, pull the knot tight.

Figure-of-Eight Bend – Parallel Ends

Occasionally used by avid climbers, the Figure-of-Eight Bend may be used wherever a quick, secure bend is required to connect two lines. Use caution, however, when loading the lines. This knot produces 90° sharp bends at the exit points from the bend. These can result in failure if dynamically loaded. Use this bend judicially.

1. Place both working ends together and start to form an underhand anticlockwise loop.

2. Take the doubled lines over the standing part and prepare to tuck them up into the initial loop.

3. Pull the working ends through the loop, completing the figure-of-eight shape.

4. Tighten the bend and fair the lines. A fairer knot will result if you put your hand loosely under the bend and pull the standing parts together so that the working ends bend at 90° to the standing parts.

Double Figure-of-Eight Bend

This bend is used by climbers and mountaineers for securing two lines together. It is most secure and has been a life-saving bend used in the most severe of conditions, including adverse temperatures, wet weather, and under shock-loading conditions. It is patterned after the Fisherman's Knot family, in that it uses two similar knots, one on each standing part, drawn together to work as one.

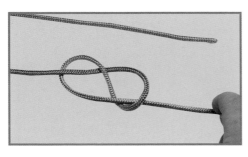

1. Form a Figure-of-Eight Knot (p34) in the end of one line, here shown in pink line. Leave a tail of about 150mm (6in) or so.

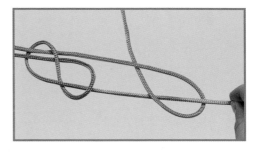

2. Pass the second line (blue) parallel to the first working end and move it beyond the first knot. Tie a clockwise underhand loop around the first standing part.

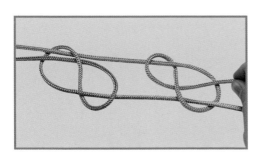

3. Complete the Figure-of-Eight Knot, passing the working end as shown above.

4. Fair the bend by pulling on both standing parts in opposite directions, so that the two Figure-of-Eight Knots marry in the centre.

Heaving Line Bend

⚓ ⚠

First appearing in print in 1912 in *De Viktigaste Knutar* by Hjalmar Ohrvall, the Heaving Line Bend is also noted in *ABOK* as knot #1463. A very secure knot, it should really be used more frequently. Instead, the Sheet Bend (p106) is more popular. The Heaving Line Bend has benefits, however, in security and it can safely be used where a greater difference in thickness between the two lines exists. Cyrus Day gives quite a different version of this bend, using instead several racking turns with a final half hitch. Both methods are good, but this version is simpler and quicker when attaching a heaving line to the eye of a large hawser.

1. Pass the working end of the smaller line over and up through the bight of the larger line to form a clockwise overhand loop.

2. Pass the working end down into the bight and bring it out beneath and to the left.

3. Bring the working end under the first pass of the standing part of the small line.

4. Squeeze the bight parts together and draw down the standing part of the small line to tighten the bend.

Shake Hands Bend

This useful and simple knot was one of many devised by the inimitable Dr Harry Asher, and deserves a high place in your knot repertoire. This bend is discussed in Roger Miles' book, *Symmetric Bends*, as 'easily adjusted or untied', a comment that is definitely borne out in practice.

Ashley in *ABOK* however, presents it as a decorative knot because of its symmetry, and ties it in a bight rather than with the working end. The knot is simplicity itself to tie, having been derived from two interlocked overhand knots.

1. First, form an overhand anticlockwise loop with one working end.

2. Insert the working end of the second line through this first loop from below. This forms the interlock of the Overhand Knot (p30) to be formed later.

3. Take the working end of the second line and form an underhand clockwise loop, passing the working end under its own standing part.

4. Focusing on the interlocking loops, steadily pass the first working end up through the open interlocked loops.

5. Pass the second working end down through this same space, crossing over the first working end. The working ends are now on opposing sides of the finished bend.

6. Fair each of the Overhand Knots and then pull all of them together to form the bend. Each working end should now lie outside the final bend.

Strop Bend

The Strop Bend or Lark's Foot is also known as a Girth Hitch, because it was used for horse tack to secure two straps together as part of the girth strapping. When climbing, however, the simplicity of this bend formed in sewn or knotted webbing, makes it ideal under psychologically stressed situations and is guaranteed to work.

Using slings or straps for attaching protection to harnesses is common in climbing, so this bend is ideal for that application. However, it results in a significant drop in strength (about 30 per cent) and should not be used when the webbing is used as an anchor or when it is dynamically loaded.

1. Open a bight to which the strop or sling is to be attached, then pass the second sling through the bight.

2. Open out the sling so that it forms an open bight, then pass the other end of the sling, unopened, through its own open bight.

3. Slip the bight up over the parts of the first bight, then start to fair the knot by pulling on the standing parts of both slings.

4. When the two slings have come together in the form of a Reef Knot (p158), ensure there are no twisted parts and tighten down.

Tips

Use this bend to secure elastic bands together to extend their overall length.

Simple Simon Double

The Simple Simon Double (part of the Simple Simon series of bends by Dr Harry Asher) seems complex from the photos, but is straightforward if you think of the action of the French Prusik style (p84) of wrapping the cord around a base, in this case the bight of the heavier line. This bend is very secure, particularly if you use a fine cord around a very heavy rope or a line of very different texture such as polypropylene or webbing, but take care to form the bend well. As shown here, you can use it with two cords of the same thickness, although there are other bends that work very well when both cords are the same.

1. Take the heavier line and form a bight, shown here in the left hand. The working end can be to either side.

2. Insert the smaller second line down into the bight and pass it around the standing part of the bight to the left and across the face of the bight to the right.

3. Continue to wrap the smaller line once more around behind the bight parts, and then start bringing it down toward its starting point. The smaller line is now wrapped twice around the bight parts.

4. Wrap the smaller line over its own parts, in front of the bight, trapping the first passes.

5. Bring the smaller line around again, repeating Step 4, bringing the working end of the smaller line again behind the bight.

6. Tuck the smaller working end up into the bight from behind, alongside its own standing part.

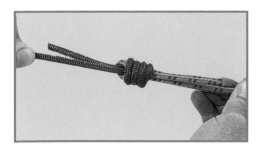

Tips

Around a heavy and slippery line, try extending the wraps – an extra turn for added security and increased friction. This bend also works well when attaching tape or webbing to regular braided line, the webbing taking the place of the smaller line.

7. Fair the bend, working the wraps down snugly, ensuring that they cross the bight in front and behind. Pull both standing parts to tighten the bend.

Zeppelin Bend

This bend, also known as the Rosendahl Bend, is one of my favourites, simply because of its simplicity and the story behind it. Apparently Lieutenant, later Vice-Admiral, Charles Rosendahl (1892–1977) insisted that this was the only bend to be used in securing airships during World War II, because it is so easy to tie and untie, yet remains secure even under the most severe forms of tugging. It was said that he would deliberately retie any other knot. Untying the bend is made easy by identifying the bights and then pushing them away from their secure location.

1. Start to form a clockwise loop by holding both lines together.

2. Take the innermost line and form a complete loop.

3. Bring the working end of the first line under the loop just formed by wrapping it around the pair of lines.

4. Bring the standing part of the second line to the right. Then, form a loop passing the working end under its own standing part.

5. Pass the second working end down into the loop and parallel to the first working end.

6. Fair the bend to completion by pulling on the standing parts and the working ends.

Tips

This bend can also be formed using opposing overhand and underhand loops placed one over the other. Turn the top working end down around the loops and up into the centre, while turning the lower working end up around the loops and down into the centre of them. To undo the bend, push the bight away from the centre and pull it out to slack.

Knots are formed in the end or length of a piece of line to create structures other than loops or stoppers. Knots are used for many purposes, and differ from hitches, bends, sinnets, lashings and loops. The special knots listed in this chapter can form the basis for other knots or stand by themselves as a useful and decorative addition to the knot-tyer's repertoire.

SPECIAL KNOTS

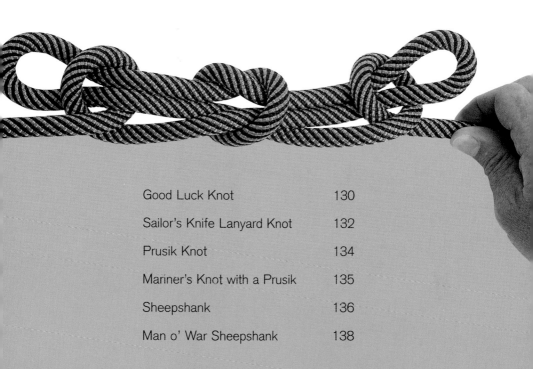

Good Luck Knot

This charming knot of Chinese origin can be tied in the hand or laid out on a table to form a decorative knot that may be attached to zipper pulls, or hung from your rear-view mirror. I have made them as adornments for bookmarks out of Chinese silk. Titled here the Good Luck Knot, the author Lydia Chen, in her book *Chinese Knotting*, states that this knot was originally nameless, although Ashley in 1944 refers to it as the Shamrock Knot. It's evidently a knot with a lucky name.

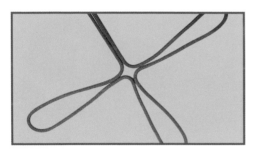

2. Middle the cord and make three bights (or four for a Lucky Shamrock).

2. Form a Crown Knot structure (p37) by folding each bight over its neighbour to one side clockwise. Keep the first fold open over your finger so that you can complete the final tuck in Step 3. You can include the parallel pair of cords as a 'bight'.

3. Make the final tuck of the last bight under the fold of the first bight where you had placed your finger, so that the knot can be tightened correctly upon completion. Here you see three bights and a standing-part pair of lines.

4. Fair the knot by pulling on each bight or strand pair until all are reasonably tight. Your knot should now look like this – almost there!

Tips

If you fold in the same direction, or from the opposite side (back side) of the knot, you will get an interesting variation.

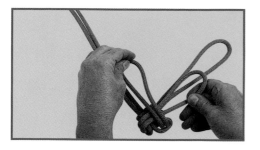

5. Repeat Steps 2–4, folding anticlockwise. Fold the leftmost bight to the right over the lowest bight, then the lowest bight up over the right-hand bight.

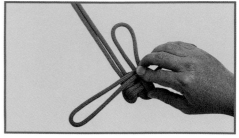

6. Fold the right-hand bight over the standing part pair and then …

7. … fold the standing-part pair down through the fold of the first bight.

8. Fair the knot to completion.

Sailor's Knife Lanyard Knot

The Sailor's Knife Lanyard Knot can be used to attach to a zipper pull on a sleeping bag, a backpack or an anorak. It is also frequently used in sailing as a release pull to a shackle or as the beginning of a Knife Lanyard through the bail of the knife, thus bringing the folding knife near to hand whenever necessary. The Lanyard Knot shown here is based on the Carrick Bend (p112) and – with a little care – can be formed in the hand.

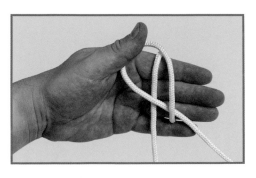

1. Pass the line over the hand from back to front. Bring the standing part up through the fingers in an underhand anticlockwise loop.

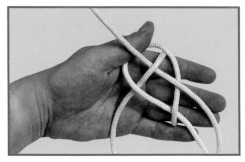

2. Bring the working end under the standing part and weave it over the loop, then under itself and over the loop again.

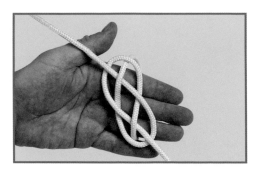

3. Fair the ends as shown.

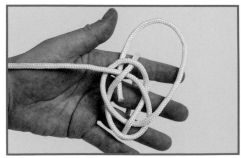

4. Pass the standing part anticlockwise up and into the centre diamond.

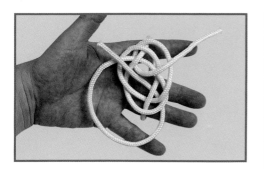

5. Pass the working end anticlockwise down and then into the centre of the diamond.

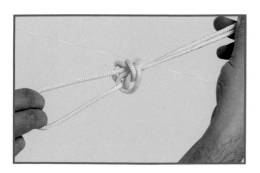

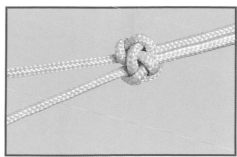

6. Slip the knot off your fingers and fair it by pulling on the bight and the two ends.

Prusik Knot

⚓ 🔺 🔺 🏠

The Prusik Knot, invented by Dr Karl Prusik in World War I was supposedly used for repairing the broken strings of musical instruments. He published the knot in 1931 in an Austrian climbing journal, and it was later popularized by speleologist 'Vertical Bill' Cuddington in the summer of 1952. It is perhaps one of the most useful knots for gripping an anchor rope, but it may slip in wet or icy conditions. Never grip the knot when it is loaded, as it may slip!

1. Form a sling (6mm; 0.2in) in polyester cord, using a Double or Triple Fisherman's Knot (pp110–111). Heatseal ends, open the sling and insert behind the anchor line.

2. Pass the knotted end of the sling through its own open loop from front to back of the anchor rope, just as you would for a Cow Hitch (p80).

3. Repeat Step 2, passing the knotted end for a second time. Be sure that the passes do not cross each other and that they lie fair.

4. After fairing, pull on the knotted part of the loop to ensure a snug fit to the anchor line.

5. The knot holds by kinking the anchor line when loaded, and relies on friction to hold after two turns. Apply more turns of the knotted ends through the loop for a Double or Triple Prusik.

6. After clipping in the carabiner, loosen the knot by pushing it, unloaded, toward the anchor. You can retighten the knot by pulling the cord in the load direction, so that the knot again kinks the anchor line.

Mariner's Knot with a Prusik

This looks at first like a hitch, but is included here because it can be used to bypass a knot in a snarled or occupied line. The Mariner's Knot can also be used as a terminal knot, temporarily taking the weight of a fallen climber. It can be tied in either cord or in webbing (tape) to produce a very effective hold during the named operation. When tying this knot, remember to maintain the tension on the sling and anchor, and do not allow too much slack to develop or it will unravel.

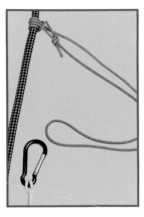

1. Attach a sling of 6mm (0.2in) cord or 12mm (0.5in) webbing around line that requires anchoring, using a Prusik Knot below the carabiner. Ensure that the webbing or carabiner anchor is secured to a separate point, and keep the joint of the Prusik sling clear.

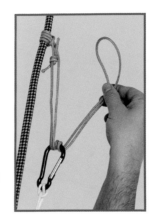

2. Pass the sling (doubled) through the carabiner from front to back. Orient your carabiner correctly, so that the gate will not be directly loaded! Pass the sling through the carabiner a second time. Be sure that the passes don't cross each other.

3. Now cross the sling from back of the carabiner to the front of the sling and start winding four or five times around the standing part of the cord.

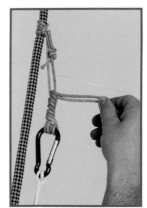

4. The knot holds by kinking the anchor line when loaded. It relies on friction to hold. Apply more turns of the knotted ends through the loop to increase the degree of friction.

Sheepshank

A most handsome and easy-to-tie knot, the sheepshank has unjustly been termed a knot only to be used for shortening a piece of rope. Try pulling the end of the rope and it will magically get shorter! This knot is also extremely useful where you want to put a line under strain but are unsure of the integrity of one or more sections. It allows you to eliminate the suspect piece from loading and to continue using the line. But beware! This knot relies on constant tension to maintain its structure. The resulting strength in maintained tension of this knot is about 80 per cent of the original strength of the line – pretty good for a defective line.

1. Form three identical underhand loops. If you make a twist right on the line, the underhand loop naturally appears. The middle loop is the one that has the suspect area of line at the top of the loop.

2. Put the middle loop over the left loop and under the right loop. Insert finger and thumb of the right hand down into the right-hand loop and pick up the right leg of the middle loop.

Tips

If you wish to ensure that the knot does not collapse, put a short length of wood into each bight formed when pulling the centre loop out. Tighten the bights down onto the pieces of wood so that some slack can be allowed in the line without the knot collapsing.

3. Insert finger and thumb of the left hand under the left-hand loop and hold the left leg of the middle loop. You now have the middle loop's legs in each hand.

4. Pull out each of the middle loop's legs to each side, left to the left and right to the right. The damaged part can be left standing a little above the knot if you wish, because it is not taking any strain.

5. Now fair the knot by pulling on each standing part of the line and be sure to keep the knot under tension.

Man o' War Sheepshank

This second version of the Sheepshank was used as a decorative knot in the 1800s. Darcy Lever (1808) and William Brady (1847), both authors of seminal seamanship books, refer to the regular Sheepshank for shortening a backstay or similar rope on a square-rigged vessel. This irregular Sheepshank appears similar to a Slipped Reef Knot tied magically in the centre of the two loops. Ashley and Graumont & Hensel each identify many sheepshank variations, but this one is more secure than the regular Sheepshank. I have as yet found very few other people who have tied this knot even once in their lifetime. Be the first on your street to do so!

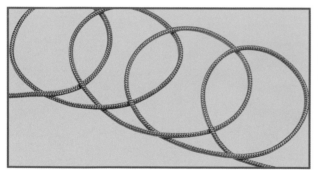

1. Form four underhand loops in a fashion similar to that for the regular Sheepshank. Position each right-hand loop over its partner to the left to resemble the line shown in the photo.

2. Focusing your attention on the two centre loops, reach down through the right-hand pair to grip the right leg of the second loop from the left.

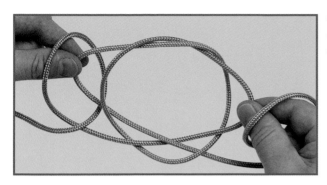

3. Reach up through the left-hand pair of loops to grip the left leg of the second loop from the right pair.

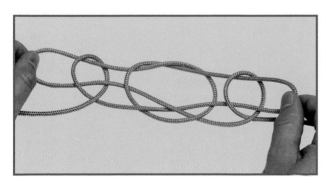

4. Holding the two legs from each of the inner loops, pull them apart slowly and carefully. You will see the Slipped Reef Knot form in the centre.

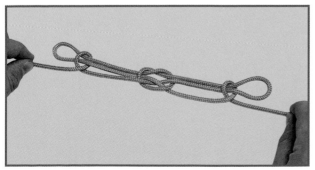

5. Pull out both the loops from the centre and fair the knot. Be sure to pull the standing part of each end of the line so that the half hitches tighten around the ends of the loops that you have pulled through.

Binding knots are used wherever you want to ensure that a line will not slip from its intended location, nor release its hold too readily. Binding knots and lashings are much like hitches. They bind lines or objects together to form a separate structure and are also used to prevent unravelling. Binding knots are not the exclusive tool of the climber, mariner, or building contractor, but are one of the most ancient and useful forms of knotting used to keep objects firmly in place.

BINDINGS

Constrictor Knot

Perhaps the most useful knot in any knot-tyer's repertoire – simple in formation and yet with the tenacity of a steel hose clamp – this knot can be tied with one or two hands and still remain firm. Its ends can be trimmed close to the knot with little or no loss of security. However, treat it carefully – with rotation it can be undone and with excessive tightening you may require a knife blade to free it.

1. Begin the knot as you would a Clove Hitch (p72) as shown here. To make a Double Constrictor, take a second turn to parallel this first crossing.

2. Complete the Clove Hitch by passing the working end parallel to the first part of the standing part, and then tucking it under the crossing.

3. Cross the working end over the parallel standing part so that the working end is off to one side of the Clove Hitch (off to the right in the photo) and ease out the standing part.

4. Tuck the working end under the standing part to the opposite side. Both working end and standing part should emerge between the two parts of the knot. Pull tight.

Tips

Try to keep all parts at the back of the knot parallel and as close as possible to each other, so that they work together to tighten down on the desired object. If the line you are using is slippery, try tucking the overhand portion a second time (a Clove Hitch–Overhand Knot combination) to form a half Surgeon's Knot.

Strangle Knot

Believed to have first appeared in print in 1916, the Strangle Knot is most lately included in Geoffrey Budworth's Tough and Versatile Knots, because it is indeed a tough knot under strain and is versatile in use. It should not be considered a tough knot to tie, however. It is readily tied in the hand and then applied to the object to be secured. Like the Constrictor Knot, this one is based on a Clove Hitch–Overhand Knot combination (Tips, p142), but the crossing is made differently. It is not as secure as the Constrictor Knot, nor can it be as readily tightened, but it is nevertheless very helpful and can be tied in ribbon, webbing or tape just as readily as in cord.

1. Start the knot as you would a Clove Hitch (p72) except that, after completing the first round turn on the right, you bring the working end across to the left side of the standing part.

2. Complete the Clove Hitch by passing the working end parallel to the first part of the standing part, and then tucking it under the crossing.

3. Cross the working end over the parallel standing part so that the working end is off to one side of the Clove Hitch (off to the left in the photo) and ease out the standing part (first pass) ready for Step **4.**

4. Tuck the working end under the standing part to the opposite side. The working end and standing part should now each emerge between the two parts of the knot. Pull tight to finish.

Boa Knot

A third in the family of binding knots based on the ubiquitous Clove Hitch–Overhand combination, the Boa Knot is firmer than the Constrictor or Strangle Knot, but not as readily secured, having more friction in its parts. Use of the Boa Knot is restricted to wet conditions where the prior two may fail. This knot easily stands up to situations where wet–dry cycling is going to occur. It also is very useful where you need to cut away the object around which it is tied very close to the knot itself (it was invented in 1996 for this purpose by Peter Collingwood, the accomplished master weaver from Britain).

1. Begin by making a clockwise overhand loop, finishing the loop with the working end pointing to the left from the six o'clock position.

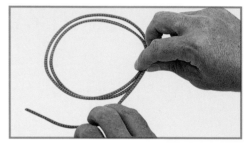

2. Add a second overhand loop on top of the first. Arrange the loops so that they lie immediately over one another.

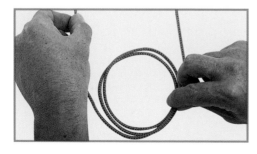

3. Bring the working end up on the left side so that you now have three parts of cord under your fingers, on the left and the right.

4. Rotate the three right parts up (away from you) by turning them over. The standing part (right) now points to you. The three parts on top now lie against the object you secure.

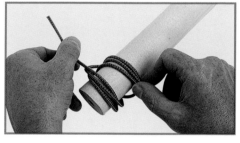

5. Start to slide the knot over the object to be tied from right to left by lifting the left and right parts together while the crossed parts slide under the object.

6. Slide the knot onto the object, and start pulling on the standing part and the working end to tighten the knot.

Tips

Take care to fair the knot so that parallel parts lie close together, else the knot will have more twists than intended, making it even more difficult to tighten.

7. Fair the knot, pulling all parts evenly and closely to the object being secured. Be careful that you follow the cord parts around the structure completely to ensure proper tightening.

Bottle Sling Knot & Asher's Equalizer

The Bottle Sling lets you secure a line around the neck of a water carrier. Dr Harry Asher invented the Equalizer to carry it with two sling handles.

The knot requires that the bottle has some kind of lip or increase in diameter, under which the knot can grip the bottle.

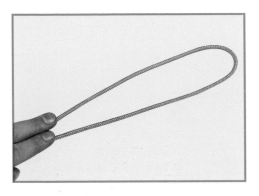

1. Make a 1m (3ft) sling and tie the ends with a Double Fisherman's Knot (p110). Pull the sling out to form a bight in the loop opposite the knot.

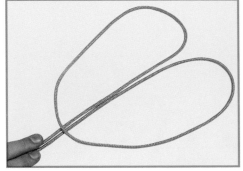

2. Open the bight and fold it back towards the knot. You should now have two loops, one upper and one lower together with a bight to the left.

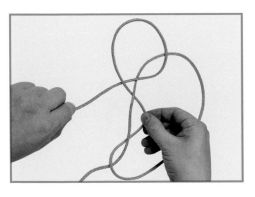

3. Slide the lower loop up over the upper loop and pull a bight from the left part of the upper loop under the left part of the lower loop (left under left).

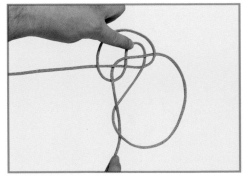

4. Move the bight up, over and then under the crossing parts as shown (left up to top).

5. Pull the bight through and over the top part of the upper loop. The upper loop will get smaller as you do this.

6. Fold the top loop down and under the whole knot by rotating your hands from a 'backs-up' position to a 'palms-up' position (round it down).

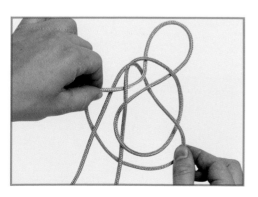

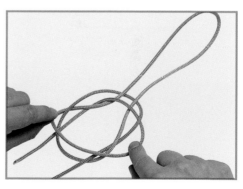

7. Shown here is the completion of Step 6 and the beginning of Step 8…

8. … which begins by folding the lower loop of the original two loops down over the knot to complete the wrap around the top of the bottle (top to bottom).

Bottle Sling Knot continued...

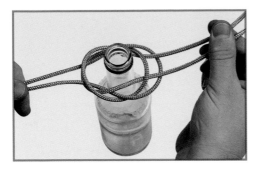

10. Draw the loop tight around the neck of the bottle or jug to ensure a secure fit. This is the Bottle Sling Knot.

9. Slip the knot over the top of the bottle.

11. Adjust the two bights so that the knotted part of the sling lies in the centre of the longer of the two loops. Bring the knotted part through the smaller bight as a bight.

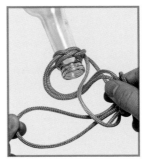

12. Open the part of the larger knotted bight opposite the knot …

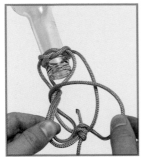

13. … and pass the knotted part through this opened bight to form a Square Knot. Pull up on this new bight to tighten the Square Knot.

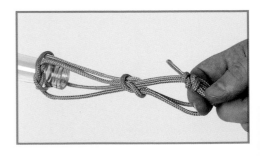

14. Final knot with Equalizer.

Double Figure-of-Eight Hitch

The Double Figure-of-Eight Hitch is so named because it is usually hitched around another object. However, it is included here because of its usefulness as a binding knot. The figure of eight is a strong structure and allows full use of twisted line without deformation or overstress. It gains its strength from the repeated crossings at the centre.

1. Start by making an underhand clockwise loop, the working end crossing under the standing part. This locks the first turn in place.

2. Continue laying the line down to form a figure of eight by making an anticlockwise loop.

3. Follow around the first loop by laying the line on top of the loop formed but without twisting the line under itself this time.

4. Complete the figure of eight with an anticlockwise turn of the working end.

5. Feed the pole or spar in under the left series of loops, crossing over the crossed parts, and entering down into the right series of loops.

6. Complete the knot by pulling on both the standing part and working end simultaneously to pull the knot tight.

Pole Lashing

Have you ever used a number of dowels, pipes or bamboo poles for a home project and wished that you could keep them together neatly? This knot will be of assistance where you want to keep a number of rod-like objects together, or where you want to secure ski poles to the roof rack. The Pole Lashing may be one of the oldest of knots in use today. Use it to tie up those loose garden poles that you used for the string beans, or to transport a bundle of pipes for your bathroom plumbing project.

1. Lay out your line and form two opposing bights. Now arrange the rods to be tied together on top of the bights.

2. Insert the working ends of each bight respectively down into the opposite bight, as shown.

3. Pull the ends away from the rods and bring them together.

4. Now secure the ends with a Reef Knot (p158).

Tips

When tying a bundle of more than six pieces together, be sure to put a cap over the ends to prevent the centre pieces from sliding out.

Miller's Knot

The Miller's Knot, also known as the Sack or Bag Knot, was used, as the name suggests, for tying bags of flour or milled oats. It is secure for that purpose, and readily tied either one-handed or two-handed. For one-handed tying, learn to form the last tuck by twisting or rolling the line while passing the working end under. This can then be tightened against the fabric of the bag.

1. First, slip the line behind the neck of the bag and cross the standing part behind the working end in front of the bag.

2. Wrapping the working end around the neck of the bag again, leave this turn slightly loose so that the working end can be passed over this part and under the first pass of the line.

3. Tuck the working end under the original standing part, so that an Overhand Knot (p30) is formed, trapping the turn made in Step 2.

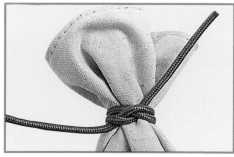

4. Fair the knot.

Sheer Lashing

If you only have two or three poles or lines to lash together, use a Sheer Lashing. It is also known as a 'seizing' (p182) when used around adjacent lines. Sheer lashings were originally used to bind together the sheer poles used when erecting the mast of a ship or when hoisting a heavy weight.

I used this lashing to bind together three sheer poles for a very strong pyramidical frame, which I then used to make fenders for a 103-year old wooden tug named *Katahdin*, now sailing in Alaska.

1. Start with a Clove Hitch (p72) tied around both poles. Keep the working end to the right, so that it can be covered by subsequent turns.

2. Trap the working end of the Clove Hitch with the first turns of your lashing. Ensure it is not lying in the gap between the poles but is caught with the turns.

3. Make enough turns to cover a distance equal to 2.5d of a single pole. If you are lashing three poles together, increase the distance to at least 3d. Tuck the final turn in between the poles.

4. Take your line at right angles to the turns and start making frapping turns by bringing the working end up between the poles.

5. Complete two frapping turns, pulling the working end tight after each one.

6. Finish the lashing by forming a half hitch around one pole …

7. … followed by yet another half hitch – to make a Clove Hitch (p72).

8. Leave a short end or tie a Figure-of-Eight Stopper Knot (p34) to prevent the line from working loose from the Clove Hitch.

Tips

Leave the lashing loose when you are securing poles for the pyramid support. Add frapping to the turns, so that the legs are able to move.

Square Lashing

This lashing can be used wherever the diagonal lashing is too rigid for the structure. There are no crossing lashings here and so it is marginally looser, because of the structure of the knot, not because of the tightness of the lines. It should not be used in tying kite frames together, because it will not stop the poles from slipping, particularly if they are plastic. Square lashings are used to this day to assemble wooden scaffolding in low-budget projects.

1. Tie a Clove Hitch (p72) around the vertical pole, and twist the working end around the pole.

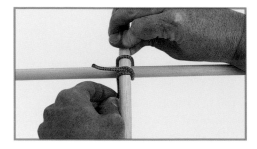

2. Make turns by weaving the line anticlockwise under, over, and under the pole parts as the line gets to each of them.

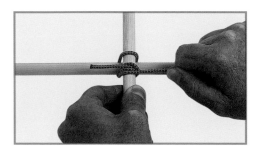

3. When you return to the starting knot, bring the line outside it to continue making the turns.

4. Make three more turns, snugging each against the preceding one so that the structure becomes firm.

Tips

If using fine twine, do not pull too hard or the lashings will break! Also, if using polypropylene or polyester, it is possible to crush hollow poles, so beware!

5. Turn the line under the last pole and start to make frapping turns clockwise around the vertical parts of the lashing, between the poles.

6. Make three frapping turns, pulling each one tight against the preceding one, between the poles.

7. Complete the three frapping turns by making a Half Hitch (p100) close up against one pole.

8. Follow up that half hitch with another, to complete the Clove Hitch with a tail of at least 12d. Leave a longer tail if you want to use the poles for latticework, so that plants have a place to which they can cling.

Diagonal Lashing

This lashing may be used where you have two poles crossing at less than 90°. It does not allow much movement of the poles. Using jute, sisal or other inexpensive fibre twines, this lashing is very useful in the garden where trelliswork needs additional support. It is also one of the few knots used in kite-making that provides firm support to the internal braces.

1. Start with the poles crossed. Form a Timber and Killick Hitch (p101) around them diagonally, pulling the hitch tight so the standing part holds fast to the loop of the Timber Hitch.

2. Take three full round turns diagonally around the junction of the poles, covering the hitch with each turn.

3. Now take the working end around under the lowest pole and start turns in the opposite direction to the first three turns.

4. Make three full turns around the pair of poles at right angles to the first three turns. Be sure to pull each turn tight.

Tips

Instead of the final Clove Hitch, use a Constrictor Knot (p142) for added security.

5. Ensure the lashings are secure by making turns between the poles, seen here moving clockwise and horizontally. Ensure that each turn is tight.

6. Complete the frapping turns by adding one or two more, depending on the tightness required.

7. Finish the frapping turns by tying a half hitch around one pole ...

8. ... and complete the lashing by adding a second half hitch – to form a Clove Hitch (p72). Pull the final Clove Hitch tight.

9. For security, add an Overhand Knot (p30), or Figure-of-Eight Knot (p34) to the working end where it exits the final Clove Hitch, or cut the working end about 2.5cm (1in) away from the Clove Hitch, so that it can't pull through.

Reef Knot

'Left over right, right over left' is the mnemonic some of us may remember from Scouting days, and the knot we formed is probably one of the most popular for people to tie. Called a Reef Knot, it is also known as Square Knot, but really forms a bend because it secures two lines together. However, it should not be used as a bend, because it can collapse into a crossed Lark's Head and completely fall apart. So why is it in the family of Binding Knots? Because it can be used as a flat knot in wound dressing, or to finish the ends of seizings. Another great application for this ubiquitous knot is to use it to bind a furled sail either above the boom of a sailboat or below the yard of a square-rigger, in a process known as reefing, hence its name Reef Knot.

1. Start by placing the left-hand working end over the right-hand working end. You may also start by placing the right-hand working end over the left one – the result is the same.

2. Twist the upper (left-hand) working end around under the lower one and bring it back to the front of the knot to form an elbow.

3. Bend the working ends toward each other. If you started by moving the left-hand working end, place the right one over the top of the new left one. Otherwise place the left-hand working end over the right one.

4. Twist the upper (right-hand) working end around under the lower one and bring it back to the front of the knot. You should now have two interlocking bights – one from the left-hand line and one from the right-hand line.

5. Fair by pulling on each working end and its corresponding standing part to close the bights together.

Tips

The collapse of this bend under strain is also a benefit to undoing it! Hold the standing part of one line and its corresponding working end. Give the working end a rapid tug away to the other side of the knot and you will have collapsed the knot into a crossed Lark's Head. Simply slide the Lark's Head off the (now straight) standing part to complete the undoing of the Reef Knot. For additional security with this knot, add an Overhand Knot (p30) to each working end around its own standing part. Never rely on this knot as a bend!

Thief Knot

The Thief and Reef knots look similar, especially when the ends are buried under the line or in the folds of a sack. A Thief Knot could be untied and, unknowingly, retied as a Reef Knot (pp158–9). The old salts' yarns reveal that a sailor could tell if someone had tampered with his bag because the unsuspecting thief had retied the wrong knot. This is an amusing binding knot and I have included it for that reason.

1. Form a bight in the left-hand cord and ensure that this first working end is on the upper side of the bight.

2. Enter the right-hand cord from below the bight; exit toward the top. Bring the working end of the right-hand cord around behind the bight.

3. Tuck the right-hand working end into the bight, adjacent to the cord's entry point. It is now opposite the first working end on the left-hand side.

4. Fair the knot by pulling on paired working ends and standing parts until the two interlocking bights come together. With the ends tucked, it is now difficult to distinguish this knot from a Reef Knot.

Transom Knot

Clifford Ashley says that he used this knot to tie together the crossed spars on his daughter's kite. Regardless of whether he invented it or not, it is a handsome knot that holds very securely for that application. It is related to the Constrictor Knot (p142), but is used where two spars or poles are to be tied together, rather than simply for tying to one rope or spar.

1. Cross the spars at right angles.

2. Begin by passing the working end over the right horizontal, behind the vertical and up over the crossing of the two spars.

3. Bring the working end across and over the standing part to trap it against the spars.

4. Pass the working end under and to the left behind the vertical spar so that it comes up on the left side.

5. Pass the working end over and under the standing part to finish on the left of the standing part. This form shows an Overhand Knot (p30) crossed by a diagonal line.

Tips

The similarity of this knot to the Constrictor (p142) and Strangle Knot (p143) is readily seen when looking at the underlying Overhand Knot. In a Constrictor Knot the diagonal binding part passes to the right over the Overhand Knot, while in a Strangle Knot it passes to the left over the Overhand Knot.

Braids, plaits and sennits are the beginning of three-dimensional string art. They are made from one or multiple pieces of line to create a patterned structure for aesthetic, if not practical purposes.

Braids lend themselves to decorative and functional knotwork. Only four examples are shown here, because this book is aimed at the outdoor enthusiast, who is searching for functionality. Plaits and sennits though can be useful as tags for zipper pulls, making them easier to find and use when your hands are cold and wet. They may also function well to prevent chafe when used as a mat. Decorative knotwork has a dual role: that of art for the sake of art, and art to satisfy function.

BRAIDS

PLAITS AND SENNITS

Chain Sennit

When an electrician needs to hang up the extension cord at the end of a day's work, when a sailor needs to temporarily put away a length of line ready for instant use, or when a child wants to make a bracelet in string, the Chain Sennit can come to the rescue very handily. The Chain Sennit has the added magic, if you will, of coming undone rather readily just by pulling on the end, yet it will stay firmly unmoved if the end is tucked through instead. This is its true value – keeping unruly lines in order, beautifully.

1. Form an overhand clockwise loop near the working end, with the standing part facing to the right.

2. Tuck a bight from left to right through the loop. Tighten the loop onto the bight to form an Overhand Knot with a Draw Loop (p31).

3. Tuck another bight up through the first and pull to close the line onto the bight.

4. Continue to tuck and pull each bight, using up all the available line, and tightening each subsequent bight after it is passed.

5. Finally, when all the line has been exhausted, tuck the working end up through the last bight to form a half hitch.

6. To remove the line from the coil, remove the last half hitch and pull the working end to release each bight one by one.

Four- or Eight-Strand Plait

Sometimes a sennit becomes a plait and sometimes a plait becomes a sennit, depending on who sees the form and from what point of view. Either way, this form of using an even number of strands to form a plaited cord produces a delightful finish that has a good 'hand' and, if made in contrasting colours, is attractive to the eye of the beholder. An even multiple of four strands makes up into either a round cross-section or a square cross-section. This version makes up into a rounded cross-section.

1. Seize four or eight strands of twine together. Use a Constrictor Knot (p142) and split the strands into two groups. Take the outer strand from the first group and bring it behind the second group. Pass this strand over and down through the middle of the second group, returning to the inside of the first group.

2. Switch to the second group, take the outer strand and bring it behind the first group. Pass the outer strand over and down through the middle of the first group, returning to the inside of the second group. Separate and tighten both groups, maintaining tension by attaching the Constrictor Knot securely to a hook or a bench vice.

3. Continue alternating from one side to the other. Always take the outer strand behind, then over and under the other strands, returning each strand to its own side of the plait again.

4. Finish the plait with another Constrictor Knot or a piece of tape to bind the ends of the strands together.

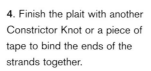

Three- or Six-Strand Plait

Three-strand plaiting is universally used to tie hair into a more manageable form. The procedure of using an odd number or multiple of an odd number of strands is similar to that of the even-numbered plaits. The final form is a flattened structure with an attractive outer edge that is pleasant to feel and see, and an intricate inner core that weaves down through the piece, giving it a feeling of fabric. As always with plaiting, it is essential to maintain an even tension and, with hair in particular, maintaining an even thickness diminishing toward the ends.

1. Tie or bind three or six strands together. If using six, form three bundles of two strands each.

2. Bring either of the outer strands over its neighbour to lie between the other two strands. Bring the outer strand on the opposite side over its neighbour to lie between the other two.

3. Repeat Step 2 for alternating sides of the plait, first left then right, until you have used the entire length of the strands.

4. Bind, the three strands together to finish the plait or finish it off with a Wall Knot (p36).

Tips

To maintain tension and ensure an even pull on all three strands, switch from one side to the other and pull on the outer strands and then the centre strand.

Turk's Head Mat

A Turk's Head is a distinct form of flat, spherical or cylindrical knot that is defined by three integers when made with one strand. We count each bight on the outer edge of the knot and each lead or change of direction across the knot. Lastly we describe the doubling, tripling or greater number of passes of each complete circumnavigation made around each knot. This flat knot is great to use as a trivet or floor mat. The knot shown here is a five-bight, three-lead, doubled Turk's Head.

1. Determine the outer circumference of the finished size. For a single pass, multiply this by three to find the length of twine. Form an over-hand clockwise loop.

2. Now bring the standing part behind this first loop to form a heart shape with the second loop.

3. Return to the working end and continue over the first loop's lower part, then under its upper part. Finish by passing over the upper part of loop (#2).

4. Tuck the first loop behind the second, then weave the work-ing end up under the first loop, over the second, under the first loop, and over the second again.

5. Following this, you should now have five bights around the perimeter. Take the working end around, following the previous line in parallel, going over where it goes over and under where it goes under, always staying on the same side as the previous line and taking care not to cross it.

Splices, whippings and seizings are not knots in themselves, but are necessary for a neat and trouble-free finish. This kind of structure also has the least effect on the tensile strength of the line.

Splicing, whipping and seizing are more effective ways of securing, extending or finishing a line, making a strop or sling in it, or creating a permanent eye, rather than tying a bend or loop in it. The smooth transition of the spliced line into itself is aesthetically pleasing, and structurally excellent. Whippings may be applied to any type of line, braided or laid, and are therefore useful in many different pursuits. Seizing of a line to a spar, pole, or to itself to form a loop, provides another method of securing line when a knot is not desirable. The splicing covered in this chapter is of the type that is used for laid or twisted line; the splicing of braided line depends heavily on knowing the construction of that particular line for the best results and is beyond the scope of this book. Splicing is usually a permanent method of weaving a line into itself and, properly made, retains as much as 97 per cent of the tensile strength of the original line.

SPLICES

WHIPPINGS AND SEIZINGS

Back Splice

A back splice prevents the unsightly appearance of a 'frayed knot' at the end of an unwhipped cut line. When made as a tapered splice it looks good, but is not suitable on the ends of lines that pass through blocks, because of the extra thickness of the rope at that point. Nevertheless, it can be substituted for a permanent stopper knot if the object through which it passes is small enough. Remember, though, to tie the splice after you pass the line through the object, or it will not fit!

1. Unlay the strands (here we used manila rope and unlaid four twists) and form a Crown Knot (p37). Pull each strand tight. Pass strand #1 from left to right under the adjacent strand in the standing part, against the lay.

2. Pass strand #3 over the adjacent strand #1 and under the next.

3. Repeat for strand #2 as for the other two strands. Take care when passing this strand, to pass it under the strand of the standing part. Pull all strands taut.

4. Starting again with strand #1. Pass it as before, but, after pulling through, untwist the strand to make it lie fair and flat against the standing part.

5. Repeat Step 4 with strand #3 …

6. … and then with strand #2. Be sure to untwist each strand as it is pulled through to make it lie fair and flat.

7. Repeat Steps 4, 5 and 6 for one more tuck in manila line (more for other types of laid fibre). When complete, roll the finished splice between the hands or underfoot if the line is large.

8. Cut away all the strands close to the point where they emerge from the splice, as shown. The splice is finished!

Eye Splice

This permanent loop at the end, or in the length of a laid line may be used to pass over a cleat, spar or branch. It can allow another line to be passed through it in order to make a rope-purchase system or a tightening loop around a coil of line. A well-made eye splice reduces the strength of the line by only five per cent and is preferred where strength is important to the finished application.

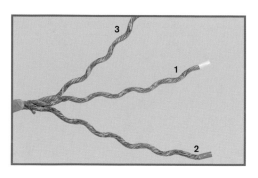

1. Open the line as for the Back Splice (p170) for the required number of tucks and add one. So for four tucks, unlay five twists.

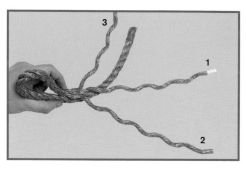

2. Turn the working end back onto itself to form a loop. Number unlaid strands from 1 to 3. Where strand #2 touches the standing part, tuck it under the standing part.

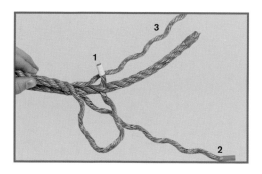

3. Tuck strands #1 to 3, in that order, under each strand of the standing part, against the lay. Here, we are tucking strand #1.

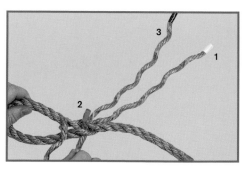

4. Tuck strand #2 of the working end under strand #2 of the standing part. These two strands lie along the centre of the splice.

5. Turn the partially formed splice over and locate the standing-part strand that lies between the two previously tucked working-end strands. Tuck the final working end-strand under the standing-part strand.

6. Follow Steps 3–5, going over the standing-part strand adjacent to the exit point of the working-end strand, and under the next strand clockwise. Untwist each strand on all remaining tucks to help the tucked strand to lie flat.

Tips

Roll the splice underfoot for a smoother surface finish. A Swedish fid will guide the strands through each of the required tucks, particularly when the line is hard-laid.

7. Taper strands by cutting half the underneath yarns of each, close to the last tuck. Tuck each half strand once more, then cut away half the remaining strand before tucking one last time.

Short Splice

The short splice is used to repair a defective line or to join two ends of identical line. If the line is to be passed through the swallow of a block, however, the long splice should be used, because the short splice will result in a local thickening of about 1.5 times the thickness of the original line. If desired, two lines of the same size but differing type (polyamide and polyester, for example) may be joined, but care should be taken to make the number of tucks appropriate to the more slippery of the two lines to be joined.

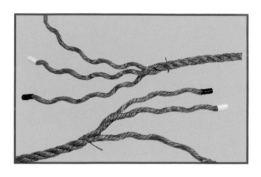

1. Unlay line ends for the appropriate number of tucks. Tape the ends of each strand to assist in tucking the strands.

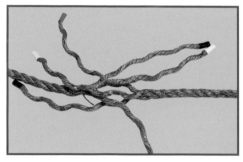

2. Marry the two lines together firmly, so that each strand fits tightly between the two strands of the opposite line.

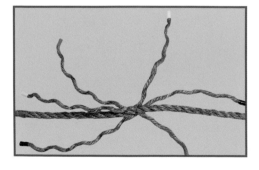

3. Tie a Constrictor Knot (p142) around the middle so that the two lines do not move relative to one another during the splicing operation.

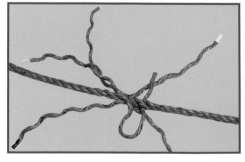

4. Pick any strand and tuck it over and under a strand in the line to be joined, tucking from right to left in right-laid line. Untwist each strand slightly.

5. Repeat Step 4 with the next strand from the same line, then repeat it with the last strand. That completes the first set of tucks for this line.

6. Now repeat Steps 4–5 for each of the remaining tucks. Then turn the lines through 180° and repeat Steps 4–5 for the second line. The splice should look as in this picture.

Tips

Remove the Constrictor Knot after all tucks have been completed and fair the splice by rolling it between your hands.

7. When all the strands are tucked and faired in both lines, cut away or taper them as for the Eye Splice (p172).

Common Whipping

The Common Whipping is the easiest to form of the many whippings available. It is sturdy, although repeated dragging of the end of the line to which it is applied may result in the collapse of the whipping, with subsequent unravelling of the whipping twine. Common Whipping may be applied to either braided or laid (twisted) line, but must, in both cases, be applied very firmly if it is to be effective and stay in place.

1. Make a long bight in the working end of the whipping twine. Hold the bight against the line with the bight near the working end of the line that is to be whipped.

2. Lock the bight of the whipping twine down with the first turn, leaving enough working end projecting to be able to grip it. This first turn should be made at about 2d of the line back from the sealed end of the line, and pass turns with the lay of the line.

Tips

On laid line, make turns with the lay, not against it, so that the laid line is made tighter by the whipping.

3. Continue to make turns with the whipping twine until a distance of 1.5d of the base line has been covered, with the bight of the whipping twine yet uncovered. Each turn should be made as tight as possible.

4. Now pass the finishing working end of the whipping twine up through the bight of twine.

5. Pull the starting working end back under the turns made so far, pulling the passed working end with it, to a point half-way along the turns.

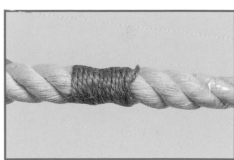

6. Trim away the working ends and the whipping is finished.

Sailmaker's Whipping

This whipping is also known in *ABOK* as the British Admiralty Whipping, being found in the *Admiralty Manual of Seamanship* (1935) and also identified as the Sailmaker's Whipping (slightly modified) in the *Manual of Elementary Seamanship* by D. Wilson-Barker (1896). It is said there this whipping is to be used on 'all earings [sic], gaskets and awning stops' or wherever one wishes to whip the end of a laid line simply, quickly and securely.

1. Unlay the strands of a laid line for about one-and-a-half turns. Double a whipping twine and trap one strand. The two parts of the bight should lie between two strands, with the bight trapping one strand. Leave the bight standing proud of the strand for a length of 2d.

2. Tie a temporary stopper knot in one part of the standing part. Twist and relay the strands back together and take the other part of the standing part around the line, in the same direction as the lay of the line.

3. Using the working end, make turns around the line with the lay all the way to the end, being sure to not trap the bight or the stopped end. The length of the whipped turns should be 1.5d of the whipped line.

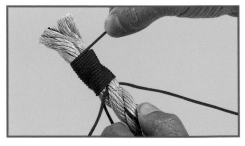

4. Continue making tight turns around the base line, until your twine reaches a point that is 1d from the end of the strands.

5. Bring the bight up from its location at the start of the whipping and open it out so that each part of it passes along the cant line of the strand it surrounds. Pass the bight over the end of the strand to the inside of the laid line.

6. Pull on the stopped end of the bight until the twine fits snugly around the top end of the strand and lies well down into the cant lines.

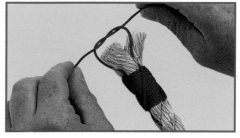

7. Lay the stopped part of the twine into the remaining empty cant line and pass it into the centre of the three strands.

8. Take the working end that was used to form the whipping and cross it into the centre of the strands also. Tie the stopped part and the working end together in a Reef Knot (p158), so that the knot lies snugly between the strands. Pull it tight.

9. Trim away the ends of the twine close against the end of the whipped line, so that they cannot be seen.

Palm and Needle Whipping

The Palm and Needle Whipping is possibly the most secure whipping available. It combines the strength of the Common and the Sailmaker's whippings, and has the added bonus that it has been stitched through the strands rather than having to rely on tension alone. It is an elegant finish and can be applied to a braided line as well as a laid line with ease. For the size of line most frequently used by the outdoorsman, this is easily the best and the most secure.

1. Thread a #14 sail-making needle with 1m (1yd 3in) twine the same thickness as the yarns of the line. Push the needle through the line's centre 2d from the sealed end.

2. Bring the doubled twine around the line so as to tighten the twine onto the line. Make sure that the twine does not twist as it passes around the line.

3. Make turns around the line for 1.5d of whipped line. Stop at a cant line and push the needle between the strands to exit between the next two strands anticlockwise.

4. From the exit point, follow the cant line with the twine, then re-enter the line with the needle and exit at the next cant line.

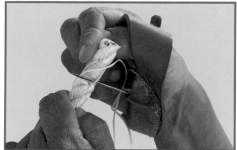

5. From the second exit point follow the cant line back to the end of the whipping and enter at the final cant line, pushing the needle straight through the line, to exit at the midpoint of the opposite strand.

6. Re-enter the needle about one yarn's thickness to one side of the strand near its exit point, passing the needle back through the strand and exiting at the cant line.

Tips

A waxed line will pass readily through the line being whipped. You could also use regular thread and rub it across a block of wax under your thumb, though not too fast or it may burn you. The twine can also be doubled for strength.

7. Make a Half Hitch (p100) around the twine that lies along the cant line and rebury the twine through the strand. Trim off the twine against the strand.

Seizings

Seizings are a way of attaching two or more lines together without having to splice, braid or knot them. When a sufficient number, length or the right kind of seizings are applied, the bond between the two lines is about as strong in tension as the original line. Because seizing twine is thicker than whipping twine, it bites into the base line without cutting into it, and enables a strong purchase to be made. The flat seizing shown here may be used to secure the working end of a line to the standing part when completing an Anchor Bend (p70) or a Round Turn and Two Half Hitches (p100).

1. Tie a Constrictor Knot (p142) around the two lines to be joined at the point where the seizing is to start. The action of seizing brings the two parts together as you progress. The length of seized line should be about 2.5d of one of the lines being seized. Leave a tail of about 150mm (6in) on the non-working end of the Constrictor Knot.

2. Bring the working end of the Constrictor Knot around the two lines, wrapping them tightly together. Apply force firmly on each turn of the seizing twine after each round turn. The squeezing action is vital to the strength of the seizing, so 'Use the Force!'

Tips

A Round Seizing is made by covering the Flat Seizing with a second layer of turns, prior to frapping the whole knot. Round seizings are used to resist abrasion.

3. When you have completed a sufficient number of turns, begin a Half Hitch (p100) around one of the lines with the twine's working end.

It is important with any seizing that you make the turns around the lines as tight as possible. If you do not have a marlinespike to tighten each turn, try using a screwdriver shaft or a clean 15cm (6in) nail instead. Be sure to pull with your whole hand over the twine, not just to one side of the twine.

4. Pass the working end between the two lines at the top and bottom of the turns and snug tight. Continue around the turns, snugging the frapping tight with each pass. Make two frapping turns in this manner.

5. Pass the other end of the Constrictor Knot that you left out originally back against the frapping turn to make a second frapping turn in the opposite direction.

6. Form a Reef Knot (p158) where the two frapping turns meet and bury it tightly inside the space between the two lines. As an alternative you may want to form two half hitches around the frapping turns, and bury them in between the two lines.

7. Trim away the ends of the twine.

Glossary

Abseil (rappel) Move down over a rock face on a rope suspended from a top anchor. Rappellers are aided by a person on belay, or may self-assist using a Munter Friction Hitch (p92).

Backup Stopper knot tied in the working end.

Belay

1. Secure one climber to another person or anchor with a line.

2. Secure a line to a cleat or belaying pin.

Bend Joining two lines by intertwining them, without splicing, or sewing.

Bight

1. Change in direction of a line of about 180°, so that the end does not cross the line but lies parallel with it.

2. Bump or other protrusion of line on the outside or inside of a knot, particularly flat knots.

Bitt Post on the deck of a vessel used to secure the end of a line.

Bitter end End of line that is not being worked, so called because it was the end that was secured to a bitt or post on a ship before the rest of the line was used for something specific like an anchor hawser.

Block Fitting used to change the direction of a line by passing the line over a sheave mounted on an axle or pin, to gain mechanical advantage.

Bollard Metal or timber post or piling to which a vessel is secured.

Braided line Lines that have been manufactured by spinning or weaving paired or grouped yarns (usually synthetic) in an over-and-under fashion, so that they spiral around the mid-section of the line in opposite directions.

Breaking strength Applied tensile force that will break a piece of line under strain. Frequently given as an average value of several breaking tests conducted by rope manufacturers. Expressed in lbs or kN as the mathematical product of the Safe Working Load (SWL) and a Safety Factor determined by the end-user.

Cable Combination of several ropes twisted together. Cable is normally left-laid, made from three right-laid ropes twisted together.

Cant line Joint between adjacent strands of a laid line, such as to form a valley between the two strands. *See also* Worming.

Carabiner Metal O- or D-shaped ring with an opening bar that is screwed home, locked in place (bent or straight gate, wire gate, twist gate, offset gate), or is not locked at all. Used to attach to a climbing harness, climbing rope, ancillary equipment like a chalk bag or attached to protection that is set in rock faces with a sling or webbing.

Cord Piece of flexible ligature, usually less than about 8mm (0.3in) in diameter, used as accessory for temporary lashing or anchoring.

Core Centre part of a line that supports the outer part and bears the majority of the load.

Cover Outer layer of a composite line, usually made to resist abrasion, where the core is made to bear the load.

Cow's tail Name given to the frayed appearance of the end of a line that has not been whipped, knotted or heat-sealed.

Crossing turn (riding turn) That portion of a knot where parts of the line, or lines, cross each other. A crossing turn is a turn made about an object where the line crosses a previous pass of the same line.

Doubling For a multi-crossing knot, doubling is achieved when the original lead is repeated alongside the original part of line with the remaining end of the line, thus giving the knot the appearance of having been made with two pieces of line adjacent to each other.

Dynamic rope Rope designed to absorb the fall of a climber, usually made with either a core of twisted line, which partially unwinds to absorb stress, or a naturally elastic fabric such as polyamide (Nylon) that will absorb stress by elongation and retraction of the individual molecules.

Elbow Two lines that are twisted around each other, each returning to the same side from which it started.

Fairing The process of drawing the individual parts of the knot tighter and aligning them into the desired shape prior to final tightening. A faired knot is one that has been shaped prior to tightening.

Fake (flake) Method of coiling a line in a series of clockwise and anticlockwise loops (figure of eight) or series of passes – from left to right, then right to left – to prevent the formation of kinks.

Fibre Threads of natural or man-made substances combined to form individual yarns.

Fid Tapered wooden pin with a blunted point, used to separate strands of a line when splicing.

Flemish Laying of a line in a continuous clockwise spiral without any crossings (Flemish Coil).

Frapping Passing a series of turns of twine or rope at right angles to tighten the original turns. Frapping is usually performed when making a seizing or lashing to tighten the primary turns.

Hanamusubi Japanese knot-tying used to create decorative articles as gifts and gift-wrapping finishes.

Hank (fox) Wrapping a line, usually twine or other small stuff, in a figure-of-eight shape around the extended thumb and little finger, with a Clove Hitch over the middle, so that the twine may be paid out gradually. As twine is paid out, the Clove Hitch is retightened to hold the hank together. Use it when you need to pass a long length of line and don't want to pull through the entire piece each time.

Heat-seal Using a small flame to sear the end of a piece of line to prevent it from unravelling.

Kernmantel Braided-cover climbing rope – the name says it all (kern = core; mantel = cover). The line diameters vary from 9.5-11mm (0.37-0.42in). The middle of a good quality rope is marked with a change in sheath pattern so as to be readily distinguishable. Normally Kernmantel is a dynamic type of rope that can absorb some of the strain of a fall. The core may be twisted or braided.

Kink (hockle) Kinks form when a line is twisted. Tightly wound loops develop that prevent the passing of line through narrow openings, which leads to rapid deterioration of the line.

Lay Direction in which the strands of a line (yarns of a strand, or fibres of a yarn) are twisted so as to form a laid part. For example, if the strands of a line, seen vertically, twist upwards and to the right, the line is right-laid and its lay is to the right. If the strands twist in the opposite direction, it is left-laid and its lay is to the left.

Leads
1. When referring to a Turk's Head knot, the number of individual crossing-line parts prior to

doubling. Also, the principal direction of a part of a knot structure at a crossing or intertwining.

2. Manner in which a line is placed so that it runs from one place to another. A lead is made so that the line does not abrade against, or over, another line or object. A foul lead is one that runs against another object or line so as to cause or receive abrasion or kinking. A fair lead is seen when a line does not abrade against another object.

Leader Thin flexible connector between the fishing line, hook or lure.

Line Flexible material used in the tying of knots, still contained on a spool or coil and not yet designated for a specific use. The diameter of line is usually greater than 8mm (0.3in).

Maedup Korean knotwork used for decoration on wedding gowns, gifts, bookmarks and other applications.

Manrope Hand line for boarding a ship along the gangplank.

Mantle Outer rope cover of a rope that resists abrasion and wet conditions.

Marlinespike (also marlinspike, or marlingspike) Tapered steel tool used by riggers, sailors and knot-tyers to splice wire rope (principally), undo tight knots and haul on lines that require tightening. The taper is known as a duck bill and is designed to slide between the strands and open them up for splicing.

Monkey's fist Three-dimensional knot, used as weight on a heaving line for throwing from a ship to the dock for docking purposes.

Monofilament Single-thickness thread usually, but not exclusively, synthetic. It is usually what constitutes fishing line. In ropework it is one of a multitude of threads used in multifilament yarns.

Multifilament Multiple thicknesses or numbers of threads of monofilament that make up the structure of yarns.

Netting needle Flat plastic or wood needle, with a width to length ratio of about 1:12. The needle has a cut-out section, allowing netting twine to be loaded in the centre for net repair.

Nip Crossing section of a knot where force is concentrated to hold or nip the parts together.

Parcelling The act of spirally wrapping a bundle of fibres, yarns, strands or line, so that they are protected and will act together. Parcelling is usually formed with strips of canvas, light tape, friction tape, or any other wrapping that does not contribute directly to the strength of the finished object, and that does allow flexibility.

Plait Weaving several lines together to form a pattern and a cohesive structure.

Quipu These coded arrangements of strings in a variety of colours and knots were used by the Incas to carry confidential information about crops, population and stores for the purpose of ensuring a complete tally of progress.

Racking Tight figure-of-eight wraps made around a pair of lines, so that neither of the lines will move with respect to the other.

Rigging Lines and ropes that hold masts and spars in place and that control the trim of sails.

Rope Generic term to describe lines thicker than about 12mm (0.5in).

Round turn Passing a line around an object to complete a rotation greater than 540 degrees.

S-laid Left-laid rope is sometimes referred to as being S-laid in professional journals and more formal descriptions. The direction of the slope of the letter 'S' shows the direction of the strands of S-laid rope. See also Z-laid.

Sailmaker's needle Triangular-section steel pin with an eye used for sewing sails or rope-work, supplied in various sizes depending on length and thickness.

Seizing Tight series of turns binding two objects.

Sennet (sinnet) Braiding using multiple strands of line so that a woven structure results. Sennets are found either as flat-woven structures or as round, half-round, square, triangular and oval cross-sections.

Service This is the covering of a line that is made with repeated turns of twine. Service is applied on top of parcelling and worming in order to provide abrasion resistance to a line and thus protect it from the elements.

Sheath Outer layer of braided line, usually provided to give greater abrasion resistance and ease of handling.

Sheet Line attached to a sail to provide the ability to change its shape (trim it).

Shock cord (bungee cord) Elastic cord used to absorb shock-loading and intended movement.

Shroud A part of the standing rigging used across the ship (athwartships) to hold a mast or spar in place.

Sling Climbing and rescue accessory, usually an endless loop formed in sewn webbing.

Slipped Tying a knot off using a bight so it may be readily spilled.

Small stuff Line less than 3mm (0.1in) diameter. In the Royal and US Navy, small stuff was reckoned to be line of less than 44mm (1.75in) in diameter, after which the line was measured by its circumference.

Spilling Release of a knot from its tied form to form a new shape or to release the parts of the knot.

Spinning Process of manufacturing ropes by means of an over-and-under construction. Machinery used in spinning is normally arranged so that the rope is produced from the centre of a rotating arrangement of spinnerets.

Splice Weaving together strands of rope to produce a homogeneous line. Splicing applied to braided line is usually achieved by enclosing one set of braided parts within the other so that the friction holds the splice together.

Standing part The part of a line that does not move during the tying of a knot or use of a line.

Static loop Term used in rock climbing to describe a permanent stitched loop in a piece of webbing or strapping.

Static rope Term used in rock climbing to describe line designed for abseiling. Static rope has little stretch and is not expected to absorb fall strains.

Stay A part of the standing rigging used on the centre line of a ship to hold a mast or spar in place fore and aft.

Stop Piece of twine turned around parts of a coil and fastened with a hitch or Reef Knot.

Stopper Any form of arresting the movement of a rope or chain by wrapping two lines in opposite directions around it.

Strand An arrangement of yarns as part of a rope or line.

String A term loosely applied to small domestic line, usually of cotton and less than 3mm (0.1in) in diameter.

Strop A length of line or webbing knotted or spliced together to form a continuous loop.

Swage Terminal end of a wire rope formed by wrapping, under extreme compression, a metal ferrule over the end.

Thump mat Woven arrangement of line used under the point of attachment of a block on the deck of a ship to prevent damage occurring to the deck by the constant thumping of the block.

Tucking Inserting one line or strand under another.

Turn Passing a line around another object or line.

Twine Braided or laid line, usually less than 3mm (0.1in) diameter.

Twisted line The form of line that results when a set of yarns or fibres are rotated about their own centre-line.

Unlay Undo or tease out the yarns and fibres of a line so that they no longer lie in their original manufactured form.

Webbing Arrangement of woven yarns formed as flat fabric, usually 20–50mm (0.8–2in) in width.

Whipping Tightly made turns around the working end of a line to prevent the line from unlaying into a cow's tail.

Working end The part of a line that you are using to form the knot.

Worming Tight laying-in of twine to the cant line of a laid line, to bring the surface of the line level for parcelling the line prior to serving over.

Yard Spar used to carry square sails across a mast on a square-rigged ship.

Yarn Arrangement of fibres twisted or laid together as one.

Z-laid Term for right-laid rope. The direction of the slope of the letter 'Z' shows the direction of the strands of Z-laid rope. *See also* S-laid.

Bibliography

Ashley, C. W. *The Ashley Book of Knots*. New York: Doubleday, 1944.

Blandford, P.W. *50 Practical and Decorative Knots You Should Know*. Pennsylvania: TAB, 1988.

Budworth, G. *Knots*. New York: Sterling, 2003.

Chen, L. *Chinese Knotting*. Taiwan: ECHO, 1982.

Day, C. L. *The Art of Knotting and Splicing*. New York: Dodd Mead, 1970.

Fry, E. C. *The Shell Combined Book of Knots and Ropework*. London: Shell UK Oil, 1977.

Graumont, R. and Hensel, J. J. *Encyclopedia of Fancy Knots and Ropework*. New York: Cornell Maritime Press, 1943.

Hensel, J. J. *The Book of Ornamental Knots*. Maryland: Cornell Maritime Press, 1990.

Hopkins, R. *Knots*. San Diego: Advantage, 2003.

Kreh, L. & Sosin, M. *Practical Fishing Knots*. New York: Crown, 1972.

Logue, F. & V. *Knots for Hikers and Backpackers*. Alabama: Menasha Ridge, 1944.

Luebben, C. *Knots for Climbers*. Colorado: Chockstone, 1993.

Pawson, D. *The Handbook of Knots*. London: Dorling Kindersley, 1998.

Raleigh, D. *Knots and Ropes for Climbers*. USA: Stackpole, 1998.

Rosenbauer, T. *The Orvis Streamside Guide to Leaders, Knots and Tippets*. New York: Lyons, 2000.

Shepherd, N. *The Complete Guide to Rope Techniques*. London: Constable, 2003.

Warner, C. *A Fresh Approach to Knotting and Ropework*. Picton: Charles Warner, 1992.

Index

Photographic Credits

1   Mike Dobel/Masterfile SA/
         Great Stock
2–3   Alain Proust/iAfrica Photos
8–9   Ben Philpott /Matson
13   Brad Wrobleski/Masterfile SA/
         Great Stock
16–17   Ben Philpott/Matson
19   Mary Evans Picture Library
20   Ben Philpott/Matson

21   Sporting Pictures
22–23   Ben Philpott/Matson
28   Ben Philpott/Matson
29   Ben Philpott/Matson
32   Ben Philpott/Matson
43   Ben Philpott/Matson
54   Ben Philpott/Matson
78   Ben Philpott/Matson
112   Ben Philpott/Matson